MW00604822

THE AMBIGUITY ADVANTAGE

The
Ambiguity
Advantage

What Great Leaders Are Great At

David J. Wilkinson

palgrave
macmillan

First published 2006 by
PALGRAVE MACMILLAN
Houndmills, Basingstoke, Hampshire RG21 6XS and
175 Fifth Avenue, New York, N.Y. 10010
Companies and representatives throughout the world

PALGRAVE MACMILLAN is the global academic imprint of the Palgrave Macmillan division of St. Martin's Press, LLC and of Palgrave Macmillan Ltd. Macmillan® is a registered trademark in the United States, United Kingdom and other countries. Palgrave is a registered trademark in the European Union and other countries.

ISBN-13: 978-1-4039-8765-5

This book is printed on paper suitable for recycling and made from fully managed and sustained forest sources.

A catalogue record for this book is available from the British Library.

A catalog record for this book is available from the Library of Congress.

10   9   8   7   6   5   4   3   2   1
15 14 13 12 11 10 09 08 07 06

Transferred to Digital Printing 2013

For my children
Claire, Niki, Yve, Meg, and Joe
who together have helped me understand ambiguity
more than any other source

Contents

List of Figures and Tables

Figures

Table

Acknowledgments

I would like to thank and acknowledge the following who have either consciously or unwittingly contributed to this project:

Sarah Smith for years of generative conversation, honest feedback, and support. Karen Lord, Tim Morley, and David Lomas at the Royal Mail Group's Innovation Lab for letting me play. Alan Robertson of Alan Robertson Associates for the truly generative and creative sessions we always have. Gordon Dodd of Alcazar Ltd for the amazing conversations turning ambiguity into physics! Sqn Ldr David Winstanley of the RAF Leadership Centre for listening and helping me understand the more rational parts of the military. I owe thanks to many people at Cranfield University, especially my staff, who have put up with my long absences and coped with the ambiguity I have provided for them, especially Janet Marshall, Emma Martin, Sally Woods, Becky Coker, Sue Henshaw, Liz Barnes, Gaynor Lloyd-Jones, and Gill Coombs. Ruth Altman for her patience. All of my students for providing much of the data that started this project. I would also like to mention the members of Cranfield's Resilience Centre whose work on disaster management and the training of disaster managers over the years has provided me with models to develop such managers, particularly Tim Randall. Also many people in the Cranfield University School of Management who have listened, often with enormous patience, to my ideas and then helped to generate new understandings in so many areas. I would also like to thank Chief Superintendent Phil Aspey of the England and Wales Police Superintendents Association for his support and encouragement over many years.

I would especially like to thank Professor Ian Davis. First, for his patience and supportive feedback when I took over his disaster management trainer training groups; second, for believing in my brand of creative development for disaster managers; and last, for developing brilliant ideas in the area of creativity in disaster manage-ment. I feel privileged to know and work with such great people.

Every effort has been made to trace all the copyright holders but if any have been inadvertently overlooked, the publishers will be pleased to make the necessary arrangements at the first opportunity.

Aristotle was famous for knowing everything. He taught that the brain exists merely to cool the blood and is not involved in the process of thinking. This is true only of certain persons. **Will Cuppy, U.S. humorist and journalist (1884–1949)**

ODE

We are the music-makers,
  And we are the dreamers of dreams,
Wandering by lone sea-breakers,
  And sitting by desolate streams;
World-losers and world-forsakers,
  On whom the pale moon gleams:
Yet we are the movers and shakers
  Of the world for ever, it seems.

With wonderful deathless ditties,
We build up the world's great cities,
  And out of a fabulous story
  We fashion an empire's glory:
One man with a dream, at pleasure,
  Shall go forth and conquer a crown;
And three with a new song's measure
  Can trample an empire down.

We, in the ages lying
  In the buried past of earth,
Built Nineveh with our sighing,
  And Babel itself with our mirth;
And o'erthrew them with prophesying
  To the old of the new world's worth;
For each age is a dream that is dying,
  Or one that is coming to birth.

A breath of our inspiration,
Is the life of each generation.
  A wondrous thing of our dreaming,
  Unearthly, impossible seeming –
The soldier, the king, and the peasant
  Are working together in one,
Till our dream shall become their present,
  And their work in the world be done.

They had no vision amazing
Of the goodly house they are raising.
  They had no divine foreshowing
  Of the land to which they are going:
But on one man's soul it hath broke,
  A light that doth not depart
And his look, or a word he hath spoken,
  Wrought flame in another man's heart.

And therefore today is thrilling,
With a past day's late fulfilling.
  And the multitudes are enlisted
  In the faith that their fathers resisted,
And, scorning the dream of tomorrow,
  Are bringing to pass, as they may,
In the world, for its joy or its sorrow,
  The dream that was scorned yesterday.

But we, with our dreaming and singing,
  Ceaseless and sorrowless we!
The glory about us clinging
  Of the glorious futures we see,
Our souls with high music ringing;
  O men! It must ever be
That we dwell, in our dreaming and singing,
  A little apart from ye.

For we are afar with the dawning
  And the suns that are not yet high,
And out of the infinite morning

Intrepid you hear us cry –
How, spite of your human scorning,
Once more God's future draws nigh,
And already goes forth the warning
That ye of the past must die.

Great hail! we cry to the comers
From the dazzling unknown shore;
Bring us hither your sun and your summers,
And renew our world as of yore;
You shall teach us your song's new numbers,
And things that we dreamt not before;
Yea, in spite of a dreamer who slumbers,
And a singer who sings no more.

In the end, we are, as O'Shaughnessy[1] observed, either part of a new world's dawning or part of an old world that is dying, and the only question for most leaders is: Which of the two worlds do you inhabit as an individual and as a leader? Are you part of the new world, with your dreams and inspiration, or are you part of the old world, which is, at this moment as you read this, being conquered and replaced even though you don't see it? Are you really a mover and shaker?

O'Shaughnessy conveys in poetry much of what this book is about: the individuals who revel in, profit from, and find the advantage in ambiguity; those who lead us into and help us navigate new worlds that are, to those of the old world, ambiguous and frightening; those who lead others through ambiguity, rather than trying to fight or control the complexity that surrounds them, with new ways of thinking that challenge the current old world conventional wisdoms. This old world is seen as comprising largely neat and ordered processes, with clean step-by-step process and management models, standardization, traditional hierarchies and organizations, a world with clear procedures and polices. The picture of reality we all know if we care or dare to look around us is actually one of chaos, constant change, fuzzy boundaries, risk taking, and ambiguity, where certainty, confidence in the conventional wisdom of the dominant group (COWDUNG), and following the rules increasingly leads to average performance, poor decisions, and business loss. The new worlds are initially places of high ambiguity.

The individuals who can truly find the advantage in ambiguity are leading the way; they are the new music-makers. They are the ones who are exploring and creating new worlds. They inherently comprehend that these new worlds of ever increasing change, where the rate of increase of change is itself increasing, are worlds of complexity and ambiguity. These emerging breeds of leaders are becoming the new movers and shakers, with their "song's new numbers" and new world thinking, who use ambiguity to create real advantage for themselves and their organizations. From these new leaders we can learn their "new numbers, and things that we dreamt not before." This book is the result of research by the author and others that helps to point the way to embrace and profit from ambiguous situations, discover and explore new worlds and new world thinking.

There are many examples of new world companies and organizations stealing the ground from under the very noses of old world established businesses, and increasingly frequent stories of large multinational companies being brought to their knees as they fail to notice a new world dawning. Those who can see the new world; those who work with and not against the complexity and paradoxes that the new world brings; who are emotionally equipped to enjoy ambiguity and who are innovative are right now creating new companies and organizations, either anew or turning around old world businesses, which are changing the face of business and work forever. They are rewriting the rules of work and society. We all have a choice, try to resist and scorn the inevitable in the knowledge "That ye of the past must die," or embrace the new world and learn their "song's new numbers." It is a choice, our choice, your choice, to either learn about the new worlds or die with the old world views.

This book presents an analysis of these new worlds and how successful new world leaders and individuals are creating these new worlds and gaining the advantage from it, while old world thinkers either don't notice that a new reality has begun, don't know what to do about it, or are just plain confused and consequently fail to act. The exploration of these new worlds – worlds where change, uncertainty, and ill definition are the norm – and the way leaders are reacting to them is illuminating and useful. Patterns have started to emerge from recent research and analysis that helps us to understand the nature of these new worlds and the nature of the people who thrive in them. These lessons are important if more people are going to come to terms with the ambiguity created by the accelerating change around them. The days of certainty and steady incremental progress are fast diminishing and, it is argued here, undesirable if we want to take the advantage. Merely coping with the increasing pace of change is not enough anymore. A person just coping with something suggests that they are reticent and under stress and probably even duress. Accepting that change is everywhere and that the pace of that change is increasing is just the start. As it is unlikely that this situation is going to reverse and that the old world of slow incremental change will be restored, rapid and unpredictable change is now the norm that we must learn to live with and not merely survive. There is a group of people who, as this work shows, flourish in such circumstances; individuals and groups who create complexity and find the creative advantage in the ambiguity that persistent change generates.

Understanding and being able to evaluate the attributes of new worlds and new world leaders and their teams can help those of us who don't naturally operate comfortably in ambiguous and new situations to learn how to move into the future of change with more confidence, learn how to gain advantage from ambiguity and hopefully actually learn to enjoy living in a world where what was is no more, and what is and will be is most likely to work by different rules than the old worlds do. "For each age is a dream that is dying, or one that is coming to birth."

Part I
How Things Appear to Be

Part I of *The Ambiguity Advantage* explores the nature and flavors of ambiguity, examining the interrelationships between risk, uncertainty, vagueness, and chaos. This examination is more than a passing or academic curiosity. The shades of ambiguity can be most helpful in diagnosing what sort of world we are facing, be it a changing old world or a new world. Also, an understanding of the range of ambiguous situations we might face can help to prevent ambiguity blindness, an affliction that many leaders face who see nothing but certainty, even in the face of what, to others, is overwhelming evidence that the rules and procedures currently being applied are out of place. You just need to examine in detail a number of leaders' responses in the U.S. to hurricane Katrina, for example the application and constant reapplication of standard operating procedures and plans that kept failing to work in circumstances that were crying out for new thinking and ways of framing the event. Evidence emerged in 2006 that the highest authorities were made aware of the possibilities of the effect of the hurricane and yet they still held to preplanned and outmoded responses for days, even in the face of increasing worldwide criticism. It appears that one of the key skills of great leaders in ambiguous situations is to acknowledge that the world has changed, and to recognize the level of ambiguity they are facing. Part I of this book examines the levels and types of ambiguity and should be read in the knowledge that what follows has no nicely packaged and clearly defined demarcation. In the world of ambiguity, boundaries are blurred and situations necessarily fuzzy. Great leaders work with it and find the advantage.

The Nature of Ambiguity

When the way comes to an end, then change – having changed, you pass through. I Ching or Book of Changes *(an ancient Chinese text)*

When the world around you changes

James Macaleese opened the car door and sat in the driver's seat. Anna, his wife, sat beside him in the passenger seat. They pulled away from the drive and headed for the city.

"Don't go the usual route," Anna suggested. "There were roadworks at the interchange yesterday and the traffic was at a standstill. It took me over an hour just to get across that bit."

James replied, "OK, I'll take the main road. It's a bit longer but the traffic usually moves quite fast and it doesn't add too much time to the journey."

"Well I'm not too sure. It's quite a fast route but there are so many accidents that I never feel safe driving along it. Also if there is an accident you can be stuck there for ages. John from next door has had two accidents on that road."

"I know what you mean, but if it is clear we can be in town within half an hour," James added.

"Actually I prefer the old road that goes through the village," suggested Anna.

"That goes all round the houses and it's a slow road," retorted James.

"I know but it's always clear," Anna continued. "It might be a bit longer and slower but you know you'll get there and it's safe. I've never heard of an accident on that road, have you?"

"No. I'm not surprised no one ever uses it, it's 'the road less traveled' and for a very good reason – it's soooo slow!"

"It's not that slow. It only adds about 25 minutes to the journey and you know that you will get into town with no hold-ups."

"I think I'll risk the main road," James said, as he pulled onto the main road. Five minutes later the traffic ground to a halt as police cars, sirens wailing, and an ambulance passed them.

"What did I tell you?" Anna said and they sat in silence.

A mile and a half along the road three cars and a goods vehicle lay smashed together, oil, fuel, and water from radiators forming puddles on the tarmac, mingling with a darker fluid slowly dripping from the center car door. Through the window, the head of an unconscious woman can be seen lolling forwards. The doors of the other vehicles are open and their shaken occupants are standing around the wreckage in silence. A police officer is trying to wrench open the car door to get to the woman. Her colleague, who has just finished summoning more help on the radio, quickly walks back to the car with a fire extinguisher and a first-aid box in his hands.

"Just in case," he says, looking at the small spiral of smoke drifting up from the engine compartment.

"I can't open the door, but she looks like she is trapped by her legs."

They both pull at the door. It finally gives way and the officers can see that the woman is trapped. They check her breathing as the ambulance arrives. The crew dismount and the four emergency service personnel have a brief chat and the ambulance crew start to examine the woman. One of the paramedics turns to one of the officers and asks if the fire service has been called, to cut the woman out.

"Yes," one of the officers responds, "but I don't know how long they will be. Is she in a bad way?"

"Pretty bad, but because of the way she is trapped, we can't get to examine her properly. As I see it we have two problems; the first is that if the car catches fire before the fire service gets here, we might not be able to contain it, nor will we be able to get her out quickly enough. We could free her but that would entail fairly major surgery on her in the car and it might not be successful as we can't see how bad her other injuries are. The second is that moving her could easily cause more problems. I would rather lift her out with the roof removed. I am really not sure what course of action would be best."

"Maybe we should aim for the worst scenario and assume that the vehicles will go up," offered the officer.

"Not sure. If we do that we could easily lose her," the paramedic replied, looking back at the car as his colleague works on the woman. Their medic cases are open on the tarmac and equipment is scattered around them like fallen leaves from a tree in fall as they work desperately to keep the critically injured woman alive.

"I'll go and check how long the fire and rescue service will be," the officer replied and ran back to her patrol car to make the enquiry.

Several miles away at the emergency services communication center, Jenny Camberly, a radio and communications officer with six years' experience, tries to contact the fire and rescue vehicle on its way to the scene of the accident.

"Alpha one base to Zulu Victor five nine, ETA (estimated time of arrival) request, over," she calls in a steady, calm, professional voice.

There is no response.

"Alpha one base to Zulu Victor five nine, ETA request, over."

Again there is no response.

"Delta three eight."

The officer replies, "Receiving, over."

"There is no reply from Zulu Victor five nine, over."

"Damn," she blurts out and shouts across at the paramedics, "sorry guys, they can't seem to contact the fire and rescue vehicle that is meant to be attending so we have no idea when they might arrive, and with the traffic backed up like this just getting through could be a problem."

One of the paramedics shouts back, "We have to get her out of here soon."

Jenny Camberly keeps trying to establish contact with the fire and rescue vehicle, "Alpha one base to Zulu Victor five nine sitrep (situation report) please," urgency now starting to enter her tone.

"Alpha base to Zulu Victor five nine, over."

"Delta three eight, there is still no reply. I'll keep trying, over."

"Roger, the situation is critical. Can another call sign respond with cutting gear, over?"

"I have requested Zulu Victor nine nine, I will get back to you when I know its ETA, over."

"Roger, thanks, Delta three eight, out."

The police officer walked quickly to the smashed vehicle and saw that one of the paramedics was now inside the rear of the car, lying on his side across the central gap between the front seats trying to access the patient from the other side. Thick black smoke billows from the front of the vehicle and the paramedics start to cough as it begins to enter the cab.

"There is still no response from the fire and rescue unit. They have requested the helicopter." The officer shouts into the car, "I think you should get out of there. I don't like the look of the smoke, it's getting worse. We could have a fire any moment," she adds urgently.

"I've got to stabilize her and this is the only way to find out what injuries she has."

"If this goes up, our combined extinguishers will only buy us a minute or so tops. I think we should do whatever it takes to get her out and take the risk."

The paramedic kneeling by the driver's door adds, "It's not our risk, it's hers and if we decide to do this, we'll have to amputate her leg here and now just to free her and in the state she's in, I doubt very much that she'd survive."

Across the city in a tenth-floor boardroom, Julian Bosworth, marketing director for a large transnational retail outlet, looks uncomfortable as he takes the board through the results of the latest marketing campaign. "I know that the trade is having a downturn at the moment, that reported consumer confidence is low, and that interest rates are relatively high, but I just don't understand why we are not having the impact we need. We have spent hundreds of thousands on this campaign, pulled out all the stops, and all the indications from our trials were very positive. Not only have we failed to arrest the drop in sales but also our market share is falling at a faster rate than ever. I am at a loss to know why. Something has happened that our normal analysis hasn't picked up. It's not as if our customers have migrated, they've simply disappeared and we can't find where they've gone as none of our competitors appear to have picked up our business. It would have been bad if they had, but at least we'd know what had happened and could set about doing something about it. It's like operating in a vacuum. At the moment I feel like we've been transported to another universe where all the normal tools of market analysis don't work. There is nothing coming up on the radar at all. If anyone has any suggestions, please be my guest."

Sanjit, one of the company's leading sales executives, decides to contribute first. "It's quite simple actually; we just need to get back to basics and apply a few simple basic rules of commerce. First we need to get a grip of our own processes and people; things have got far too complex and, if I may say so, out of hand in this company. We have managers listening to what the workers want instead of the other way around. I would certainly sack a few of the worst performers and reward some of our best to get the message across about the level of performance we require and create some order around here. We also need to make our products more competitive. We have been going for creative instead of following the rules of the game with some tried and tested products that have always worked. All these newfangled ideas are just confusing people. Personally getting back to good old-fashioned values and some strong leadership is what we need. It was always the right way in the past and it's the right way now."

"That's all very well but this is a new situation and following the old rules just won't work that simply," argues Elizabeth, the head of advertising. "Life is a little more complex than doing what we have always done and simply following 'the rules.'" Elizabeth punctuates the words "the rules" by drawing the quotation marks with two fingers on each hand in the air. "We really need to explore the possibilities of the current market. Far from simplifying things, we must explore the possibilities by properly analyzing the situation. It is important that we listen to our people and our customers. In short, we have to change, not go backwards, we have to adapt to market conditions and seek out the opportunities that will allow us to prevail. I am not saying Sanjit is wrong or anything, it's just that I think that we should explore other ways to see what works."

Joy, head of purchasing, speaks next. "As you all know, I have been in this business quite a few years and I have seen ideas come and go and quite often come around again. For me, the key is in the way we are perceived both internally and externally. Things are moving fast out there and we are a large organization. I think that rather than control things from the center, as we have tended to do in the past, it might just be an idea to empower our regions to make the changes that they, in their experience, need to. We have got to trust our managers in the regions and if that means having different campaigns in different areas, then fine. If, on the back of that, we promote more of a family atmosphere in the company, capitalizing on the strengths of our people and supporting our managers to take business risks and respond to local conditions, I think we will do a lot better. You see, at the moment, we have our sales teams competing with each other. It's daft, they should be working together, sharing resources and ideas, not keeping information from each other. And then, if it were up to me, I would tweak the company so that it reflected the values of today. For example, make a statement about not using far eastern sweatshop production lines. Doing the fair trade thing would help for a start and using renewable materials, would show our customers that we care. That would work and would get us out of the 'cutting costs to improve the bottom line' syndrome. Cutting waste is how I would prefer to see it and I think our employees and customers would too."

Lastly Chris, head of innovation, contributes. "I have been wondering if there are other people outside the board we should be bringing in on this? To be quite honest, I'm not sure that we even know what the problem is. We think we know but I've been thinking that we are seeing the symptoms as the problem. Our reduced market share and slow sales are not the problem. They are, I think, a symptom of a deeper problem that needs exploring before we start on a solution. There may not even be one solution to this. I suspect that there may well be elements of each of our solutions that can be brought to bear on this issue. None of what we have been discussing is mutually exclusive. The point for me is that clearly these are different times and they require different thinking."

There are discernable delineations between the range or type of certainty each situation presents. While not always immediately obvious to individuals, these delineations are accessible to those who care to look. There is the certainty of the old world that we understand and that can largely be predicted with a comforting degree of confidence. Calculable risks on the other hand, introduce a level of uncertainty and choice. The choice and uncertainty of which way to turn, which decision to make or path to take, weighing up the possible consequences. As uncertainty increases, there are those situations where we do not know what might happen next, either because we have gaps in our knowledge or we know a lot about the situation. However, what is known has come together in such a unique combination that we are uncertain as to what might happen in this new composition or situation. Then there are those situations that appear to be roughly familiar, but not quite, where things appear to be the same but strangely different, where what we do doesn't quite have the effect we expected, and somehow understanding the order of things appears to be elusive. Lastly, there are such new situations where all the old rules and knowledge count for nothing: those situations when everything you predict or expect to happen breaks down completely. It's as if you have landed on a new planet with new rules – total ambiguity or chaos. Risk, uncertainty, vagueness, and chaos, or ever increasing levels of ambiguity are part of everyone's life. Every individual, every group, team, company, organization, country, and species have, as part of their world, shades of the unknown. From the calculable gamble of this or that decision, right up to extinction threatening new world situations where all bets are off, where survival has become the predominant occupation and our current knowledge, thinking, values, beliefs, and behavior don't contribute to solving the presenting problem; situations where only the most adaptable and imaginative survive and move through to help develop the knowledge, thinking, values, beliefs, and behaviors of the new world.

Old world thinking in a new world

One of America's most successful companies struggled and finally went into receivership when the world around it changed out of all recognition in 2000/2001. Only saved from total extinction by new world thinkers outside the company some years after entering a coma, Polaroid now lives with new knowledge and understandings appropriate to the new digital world. The ambiguity created by changes in photographic processing business models and the rapid expansion of digital camera technology caused confusion followed by denial of the problem, a series of bad decisions (old rules, values, beliefs, and thinking applied in a new world), and finally panic by the

Polaroid Corporation, which was eventually brought down when it entered receivership in October 2001.

Polaroid was founded in 1937 by Edwin H. Land, a Harvard dropout who left the university aged 17, continued his own research into polarization and then set up the company founded on the manufacture of sunglasses, 3-D glasses, desk lamps, and filters for gun sights. During World War II it even developed a heat-seeking missile years ahead of its time. On February 21, 1947 Land amazed the Optical Society of America meeting in New York City when he demonstrated his single-step photographic process that enabled pictures to be developed in only one minute. The following year, Polaroid marketed the world's first instant camera and film that was to become the company's flagship product line.

All was well until a new world beckoned, with the advent of the digital camera and new photo processing technologies. Initially the response of the corporation to this new world was to ignore it, believing that the markets of digital photography and its own instant products were defined differently enough not to affect sales. The first signs of the new world arrived in the form of the widespread availability of local processing labs whereby every corner shop and chemist could offer reasonably priced, fast processing within the hour, which began to hit sales of the Polaroid camera and film by the late 1990s. This was further compounded by the advance of digital imaging technology in the late 1990s/early 2000, which further hit instant imaging sales. Initially, overconfidence[1] – the application of old world rules and thinking in a new world scenario by what had been considered until now to be one of the most stable and innovative companies in the world – doomed it to inactivity or, more correctly, the wrong activity.

When the new world was finally recognized via the useful corporate "new world recognition tool" of falling sales and reduced profits in 2001, a change in strategy was instigated, using old world Polaroid values of homegrown innovation and the development of entirely new technology. This fatally slowed its response, which was already lagging behind the competition, and increased the costs beyond its ability to develop and bring to market its solution. The following small article appeared in the *Boston News* in the USA.

May 31, 2001

Polaroid Pins Hopes on New Products

By Thor Olavsrud

NEW YORK – Thanks largely to the instant gratification offered by digital cameras, Polaroid sees a difficult future for film sales – a staple of its business – but that doesn't mean the inventor of instant photography should be counted out just yet.

Noting the lack of attention that's been paid to improving the creation of hard copy prints of digital images, Polaroid has unveiled two new technologies, which it hopes will make it the standard-bearer for the digital printing industry.

Code-named "Opal" and "Onyx," Polaroid is looking to these technologies to take itself beyond its heritage of silver halide-based film.

"The Opal and Onyx technologies will revolutionize how we move digital images from pixels to prints," said Gary T. DiCamillo, Polaroid's chairman and CEO. "These are real game changers – true innovations that will set new standards for instant digital printing quality, mobility and affordability."

By September of the same year, the following report was filed online by *The Imaging Resource*.[2]

Polaroid's Problems Persist!

By Michael R. Tomkins, *The Imaging Resource*

80-year-old company considers sale – but will buyers be lining up or shying away?

Polaroid Corp., probably among the most famous names in the photographic world, has had a very troubling time over the last week. Speculation began last Wednesday as the company reportedly considered filing for bankruptcy to gain protection from creditors, as it approached the expiration of a $360 million line of credit. Shares which were trading at almost $20 a year ago plummeted by 46 percent on Wednesday to the stock's lowest price in 10 years, trading at a low of $1.45 before closing at $1.87.

As the market closed, Polaroid announced that it had reached agreement with lenders to waive certain bank loan covenants through October 12, 2001, and a $19 million principal repayment that was scheduled for September 2001.

The company also announced it would fail to make interest payments of $11 million due July 16, 2001 on its 6.75 percent bond notes maturing on January 15, 2002 and its 7.25 percent notes maturing on January 15, 2007, as well as a $16 million interest payment due August 15, 2001 on its 11.5 percent notes maturing February 15, 2006. The press release noted that Polaroid would begin discussion with bondholders to restructure its debt, and had retained Dresdner Kleinwort Wasserstein and Zolfo Cooper LLC to assist in the negotiations.

Reports of vultures circling the dying company started to abound; for example, a Reuters report identified a number of companies who might be potentially interested in buying the now near-extinct company. The report concluded that rivals Eastman Kodak Co. and Fuji Photo Film Co. Ltd. would not be attracted to Polaroid's brand name, but might find the company's patent portfolio interesting. It was also speculated that equity firm Schroder Ventures, which attempted to buy Belgian imaging company Agfa-Gevaert N.V., may be interested in using the Polaroid brand; the company had shown interest in Agfa's brand name in talks with that company but the deal fell through when it couldn't secure rights to use the Agfa name.

Canon Inc., Sony Corp., and Olympus Optical Co. (a company which had cooperated with Polaroid in the past) were also suggested as potential suitors, although it was felt that Polaroid's instant printing technologies might directly conflict with their digital camera lines. It was now believed that a different approach by Polaroid, rather than trying to reinvent digital technology late in the day, could have "bolted-on" existing technologies to profit from the best of both worlds, producing small fast prints from digital cameras, which incidentally is just the technology which is currently emerging – small personal photo printers for digital camera users.

Its old world response to the ambiguity created by the advent of the new world of the digital revolution cost the company dear. Sadly for Polaroid and its shareholders, the realization about the possibilities and impact of digital imaging on the home market was too late. Having patented the new "Opal" and "Onyx" technologies, the corporation didn't have the funds or the time to develop the ideas and bring them to market. Barely ten years after its creator, the flexible and inventive Land, died, so did his corporation, a victim of a new order. The company went into receivership on October 12, 2001, with hundreds of millions of dollars of debts, leaving shareholders, employees and retired workers with nothing. A holding company was formed and most of Polaroid's assets were taken over by Bank One in America, until April 27, 2005 when the Petters Group Worldwide announced its acquisition of the Polaroid Holding Company.

So why did a corporation that was once part of the Nifty Fifty (Polaroid had the reputation of being a member of one of the fifty most prosperous companies in the United States) fail so badly in the new digital world? Being a Nifty Fifty ranks a company as one of the most desirable to invest in because it displays innovative ideas and effective managerial practices.

Why is it that innovation and effective management isn't enough to guarantee success? What happens when the world changes and condemns the progressive thinking and practices of one era to the trash can of a new order in a very short time? Time and again examples from corporate, government, and personal arenas show similar patterns. The thinking that thrives in one set of conditions quickly causes a crisis when those conditions change or a problem is encountered that the current system of thinking cannot understand and solve.

A number of failings can be discerned from Polaroid and other, similar cases such as Ford, IBM, and Xerox for example. First, as most dinosaurs find, new world scenarios happen catastrophically fast, at least from the perspective of old world thinkers. Because old world thinkers are viewing and analyzing everything from an old world perspective, they frequently fail to see alternative explanations and interpretations, effectively filtering out the new world. Once new world thinking is applied, it becomes obvious just how long the trail of warnings were, but old world thinkers can't see the warnings at the time, as their thinking frames usually prevent it.

Polaroid, like IBM, Ford, and others, ignored or denied the

importance of data, like falling sales, reduced share prices, and market share which should have alerted them to the possibility of the presence of a new world. The "this isn't happening" or "yes, but look at how good we have been" mentality is a killer every time. Listening, looking, and thinking, and then double-checking what you have seen, heard, and thought with another source always beats arrogance and plowing ahead "because we are really good". Focus and application is good when you need to complete a task. The same traits that are successful in completing tasks can spell disaster strategically when a new world is dawning, simply because you are blinkered to the possibility of a different world of different interpretations and different meanings existing.

Second, having rules and sticking to them in the face of changing conditions, when you find yourself in a new situation, is problematic enough. Where the rules aren't working, making the rules even tighter or more rigid rarely works. If the current rules aren't working, there could be a good reason – so try new ones. Polaroid's visionary management structure and processes of the 1970s – which put it into the Nifty Fifty and became the rules of "how we manage around here" – were just right for that world. However, it stuck to the rules in the face of ambiguous times and lost. Similarly, during the 1990s at Ford, before they nearly went bust, there was a policy of automatically firing anyone with low performance appraisal scores. This so affected the climate in the company that entrepreneurial risk taking died overnight.

A reverse situation occurred in the UK Foreign and Commonwealth Office in the 1980s and 90s. It profiled the most successful high flyers and recruited new staff and appraised existing civil servants against the model based on the best of the best. It didn't take too long for all the oddball civil servants and those who didn't fit the mold to be rooted out or become an endangered species and for an organization of like-minded high performers to emerge. It also didn't take too long for the lack of diversity and challenge from the creative oddball characters within the organization to begin to show, with a series of ill-considered actions, stifling bureaucracy, and internal "mistakes," enough to embarrass any government into change. Such examples of set rules-based thinking include the following from a 1994 interview with an unnamed British businessman quoted in *The Scourging of Iraq* by Geoff Simons,[3] when he describes the tortuous process of attempting to send medical supplies to Iraq:

Before any individual or company can talk to an Iraqi buyer, they must apply for a license to negotiate. Licenses to negotiate can take three to four weeks to issue. Only when the license is issued can you start talking without breaking the law. Once the buyer and seller agree [a price] the seller must then apply for a supply license, which can take up to twenty weeks to issue. In the meantime the Iraqi Dinar is suffering daily devaluation and inflation beyond control. Twenty weeks later the seller receives the supply license by which time the buyer's situation has changed. This forces the buyer to cancel the order, or, at best, reduce the quality or quantity of the goods in order to raise the hard currency needed to finance the purchase. But [the Sanctions Committee insist that] any change to the application means that the entire process must start again.

Rules are fine but if the conditions change, sticking to or reinforcing the rules won't change things back or solve the problems in a new reality. New realities require new rules.

Third, knowing and believing in something (intellectual capital) isn't enough in the face of a new world. The collective wisdom of Polaroid was great, it knew how to invent new things, sell them, and make a profit in the old world order. However, operating in an as yet unexplored and therefore highly ambiguous world, with the knowledge and thinking of yesterday, and sometimes even today's knowledge and thinking, will often count for very little. Indeed, the old world knowledge you have is quite likely to be your downfall. IBM, Xerox, and many others found this out to their cost. The world changed and they nearly died. IBM's leaders, for example, were attached to the high prices and huge gross margins, as well as their positions, earnings and status that came with the thinking "we do really big computers." The "big computers are where the big money is and we are great and innovative with big computers" thinking paradigm meant that that they could not accept the end of the mainframe era even though they were starting to have massive sales success in the PC arena – PCs were a sideshow. Unfortunately for IBM it couldn't initially see that a new age had dawned. Like Polaroid and Xerox, IBM hadn't cottoned on to the fact that real intellectual capital is founded on intellectual curiosity and intellectual and institutional change and not on static notions of knowledge. The world may appear one way to you but the data may suggest other things – explore them. Chapters 8 and 9 explore this matter further and show how to develop these within your own area of influence.

Fourth, failing to realize that thinking, innovation, and creativity are context-dependant is another problem often faced by established companies and thinking. When we try to solve a problem, we do so with thinking and rationale that is bounded by our understanding of the way the world works now. This is great and keeps working as long as the world works in the way we think it does. The moment a new world order comes along or more likely a problem that cannot be satisfactorily solved in the current world view, then a new thinking paradigm or vMEME (discussed later in the chapter) is required to even construct the problem adequately, let alone solve it.

Fifth, managers got to be managers because they were good at dealing with and solving problems back then with the thinking systems of back then when they worked. Just because they were good then and might even be good now, does not mean that they will be good when things change. The same applies to leaders. If the world changes, it is very likely that the thinking, values, and beliefs have to change too. We often need to reappraise who are our good managers and leaders in new world situations. Past performance is not neces-sarily a good predictor of future performance for many people in new world situations.

The Polaroid story can be contrasted with other industries that survived a sudden change in world conditions affecting their business by using a different thinking system when required.

Attributes of the old world in the new world's order

Before starting to explore the nature of new worlds and things that many of us have "dreamt not before", an examination of the types of assumptions that much old world thinking is based on, and are currently being challenged by new world thinkers, particularly in organizations, will serve as a useful example to help to clarify and distinguish the current differences between the two forms of thinking, and in particular the beliefs they are founded on.

At this time it is normal to cluster business and work practice around the concept of "organization." We work and think in terms of organizations, companies, partnerships, institutions, and the like, which carry with them the presupposition of intentional, organized, and rational order, moving, usually in a linear fashion, inexorably towards some form of goal or mission. I would like to begin by highlighting the ten basic assumptions that underpin current world thinking, assumptions that are being questioned by the new world thinking that is being created as I write. These are the assumptions of:

1   Cause

2   Order

3   Choice

4   Motivation

5   Capability

6   Development

7   Position

8   Problem

9   Movement

10   Logic

Assumption 1: The assumption of cause

The assumption of cause is that everything has a direct causal relationship with something else and that we just need to discover what that relationship is to find the rules to apply in any situation.[4] This is predicated on the idea of cause and effect, largely conceived as a Newtonian construct. The idea is that every effect has a cause, and that if we look hard enough, scientifically enough, and with the right tools, we will discover what the cause is, and if we can control the cause, we will therefore also manipulate the effect. This is based on two further assumptions; first, that we can truly ever find a cause to something and second, that the relationship between the cause and the effect has some form of rational and direct association. This then gives rise to the notion that if we manipulate the cause, we will alter the effect in the direction we intended. Public policy is littered with enough examples to convince even the most hardened skeptics of the folly of these assumptions, and yet whole organizations and departments like human resources are based on this very assumption. As the task of discovering cause and effect gets ever more elusive, especially as far as controlling human beings is concerned, the larger these departments and organizations become. If such cause and effect thinking was working, the question is, why are we witnessing an increase in such endeavors?

Assumption 2: The assumption of order

The assumption of order has two elements. The first is linked to the assumption of cause, in that the relationships between a cause and effect are assumed to have some form of reasonably fixed order; do X and Y will happen. This then feeds the second assumption of order, which is that order is required for productivity, development, and understanding; as mentioned above, it is no mistake that we give the collectives we work in names that suggest order, names such as organization, institution, company, partnership, and so on. This also has the effect of adding value to the idea of order; order is good, disorder or chaos is bad. Just think about the normal usage of the word "chaotic." It is rarely used in a positive context. The question is, is such an assumption axiomatic?

Assumption 3: The assumption of choice

The assumption of choice states that people's actions are usually assumed to be made as a result of logical decision making. That the actions of other individuals, competitors, organizations, and so on and their constituent decisions are assumed to be wholly intentional, and that the choices others make are assumed to be considered, positive, deliberate choices. We rarely attribute mistakes or a lack of intention in others' choices. It is worth asking what effect this has on decision making and relationships.

Assumption 4: The assumption of motivation

Linked to the assumption of choice is the assumption of motivation; that choices are intentional and genuine choices. As mentioned above, we assume there is a positive motivation behind others' choices. There is another assumption of motivation in old world thinking; that an individual's, group's, or organization's motivation can be understood and therefore manipulated – that we can do X to have the other person do Y. Much of management theory is based on this assumption. The assumption of motivation assumes that motivation is a logical and causal entity that can be manipulated to suit the ends of the "motivator."

Assumption 5: The assumption of capability

The assumptions here are, first, that the acquisition of capability indicates the intention to use it and, second, that we know which capabilities will be needed in the future. Just because someone or some organization has the capability to do some act does not mean that they will fulfill that capability, nor does it mean that their will or goal is to fulfill it. A further consideration here is that by definition most organizations' capability maps, grids, or lists are based on current perceived wisdom about what has worked well in the past. They are largely historical in nature and are rarely, if ever, future paced for emerging scenarios. Additionally, concepts of capability are usually envisaged within restrictive thinking systems.

Assumption 6: The assumption of development

The assumption here is threefold. The first is that development *will* occur. Even if specific training is directed at an issue, it does not mean that the training will result in change or action as predicted. Indeed, most training and development programs have poor evidence of development leading to the predicted action. The second assumption is that development is unidirectional, that is, it can only help or make things better. While the intention may be exactly that, the assumption that intention and reality are the same is just that, an assumption only. The third assumption of development is that this takes place in some form of incremental and linear fashion, that there are well-defined foundations to development either at the individual, group, or organizational levels. Development plans are almost always based on these assumptions, with little evidence that this is any more than an assumption.

Assumption 7: The assumption of position

Simply, the assumption of position is that the individuals, groups, or organizations hold a position or rank in the world, either hierarchical or social, and that those positions are held for a rational or good reason and that that reason still applies. The suggestion of this assumption is that position is real, it has form and is treated as such, a reality rather than a perception. This leads to the notion that hierarchical leaders cannot be challenged and that they have real power rather than that given up to them.

Assumption 8: The assumption of problem

The assumption here is that when we perceive a problem it actually exists in reality. Further, what we also perceive about the problem, its nature, its boundaries, and the limitations we perceive become real and tangible. What this means is that the moment we notice a problem, it suddenly comes into existence and becomes our reality. The result of this is that the problem that has become our reality is "the problem." It may not be the problem at all, it could be an illusion, a symptom, or an impression of some other issue. This is of course an assumption.

Assumption 9: The assumption of movement

The assumptions of movement are that there has to be movement and that we can control the direction of any movement of any individual, group, organization or market.

Assumption 10: The assumption of logic

Simply put, this assumption is that most of what happens has a logic underpinning it, that logic is linear and positive, that it moves in one direction (positively), and that all presented logic can be understood using our current understanding and thinking, otherwise it is not considered to be logical.

These assumptions are seldom considered when problems are being solved and decisions made. They are important factors in old world thinking systems. As such, they are being challenged in the most robust manner as new world companies rise and start to take over as change grows apace.

In short, old worlds usually operate in some semblance of order and reasonable certainty. The likelihood of the presence of a new world increases the closer to full ambiguity or chaos the situation appears to be. Unfortunately many will not be able to see the ambiguity present, being addicted to the certainty and order that will keep them blind to any new world dawning. The assumptions above contribute to this blindness and increase the level of ambiguity felt when the world changes.

Ambiguity, vagueness, uncertainty, and risk – the ambiguity continuum

To be able to recognize the possibility of a new world's arrival or to understand what sort of problem we might be facing, it is important be able to grasp the level of ambiguity we are facing in any situation (Figure 2.1). Comprehension of the level of ambiguity will inform us what possibilities exist and help us to decide what actions to take in any situation.

In the worlds of decision making, engineering, finance, and economics, for example, the terms "risk" and "uncertainty" have definite meanings; the definitions of which are important to those disciplines and contribute to how practitioners envisage the concept of ambiguity. Additionally, the meanings and associated emotions connected to each of the concepts are grounded in the context and discipline it is viewed from. Here we are about understanding the

nature of ambiguity and how we all might seek the advantages
inherent in ambiguous situations and contexts. To this end it is useful
to think about what ambiguity is in the context of other forms of
uncertainty. Much of what follows has been informed by the work of
Paul Schoemaker[5] but differs in quite systemic and crucial ways.

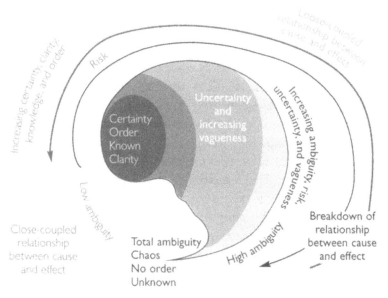

Figure 2.1 The ambiguity continuum

Certainty

This is a theoretical state where we have all the possible data and can
predict with total accuracy the results of any action or actions.
Indeed, certainty brings with it the proposition that the future is foreseeable in some form of scientific manner. There are no problems in
such a condition, only assurance, which is why this is a theoretical
state. While at a low level of abstraction, certainty might appear to
exist, for example agreement that the object in front of us is a tree,
however, beyond such agreement and at higher levels of abstraction,
certainty becomes much more elusive, as do the associated constructs
of knowledge and fact. Classical philosophy distinguishes between
knowledge and belief, where certainty, knowledge, and fact were seen
as parallel constructs, and the drive for certainty was traditionally
seen as one of transcending belief. As we shall see in Chapter 3, an
exploration of complexity shows that current understandings of

knowledge are both somewhat less and yet better defined than they were in John Dewey's time (1933).[6] Needless to say, certainty is a rather slippery concept and contains a series of apparent contradictions, most of which are philosophical and do not concern us here. However, practically, if one thinks about it, there is a paradox contained here, if we are certain we know what has happened and what will happen. Since the ideal of certainty, to know and be able to predict with total assurance, is not achievable at any useful level of abstraction, the belief that we are certain about anything is necessarily just that, a belief, not knowledge. Beliefs can reduce our search for reality if they are confused with valid and reliable evidence, and not seen as a hypothesis to test. However, certainty is not belief and being certain therefore does not have the inherent inquiring basis that knowledgeable belief does. In fact, certainty blinds the certain to the possibilities inherent in any situation. Thus the paradox is complete; immutable certainty masks ambiguous reality and therefore the possibilities inherent in any situation. Anything that is not certain must consequently be ambiguous, and the level of ambiguity increases as we move from low-level risk through high risk and uncertainty, vagueness, and finally into chaos or total ambiguity. What follows is an exploration of the (nonlinear) continuum, with the dual theoretical concepts of absolute certainty (certainty) and total chaos or ambiguity at each end (see Figure 2.1 above). Here ambiguity describes all that is not certain. The interrelated, coexistent, and increasing levels or shades of ambiguity – risk, uncertainty, vagueness, and chaos – are discussed below.

Risk

Risk refers to those events where the probability of something happening can, to some extent and with varying degrees of confidence (confidence interval), be calculated. So, for example, the chance of pulling the ace of spades from a deck of playing cards would be seen as a risk, as there is a 1 in 52 chance of getting the card you want, assuming a normal deck of cards and an "honest" choice, of course. We may not "know" that we will get the card we want, we can however work out the probability of such an event and make a decision based on that probability. The probability or risk of getting any one particular card from a deck is 1 in 52. Insurance companies work on a calculation of risk, the risk of not making a profit on a particular event. They will examine and quantify any factor which affects that risk, so for car insurance for instance, how attractive is the car to thieves, is the area it is left in unattended, in a high or low crime area, is it secured? In our everyday lives, we make this sort of calculation every day. We weigh up the risks of being caught speeding, or having an accident while driving or flying. Employees sometimes take the risk of being sacked or disciplined by misusing company assets; we weigh up the risk of having a seriously good meal in a particular restaurant. We take a risk when we get a new haircut, for example, and we try to minimize that risk by not just walking up to anyone in the street and asking them to cut our hair. We find hairdressers that we like so as to reduce the risk of a bad job. In each of these cases, we know what we know and don't know, and take steps to reduce the elements of doubt as much as possible. As the amount of calculable data we have about the situation decreases, the level of risk increases.

Some people are better at calculating risk than others, and in certain contexts some appear to be overcautious, and others come across at times as imprudent "risk takers." Just driving a car at 30mph for some is a perceived as a huge risk, while others don't even sense a risk in riding a motorcycle at high speed along narrow country lanes. While the risk of an accident in each case is different and reasonably calculable, individuals' perceptions of the actual value of the risk are quite different. Additionally, it is important to realize that just because a risk is calculable does not mean that it has been calculated. So maybe the motorcyclist who is riding really fast along small country lanes has as little appreciation of the risk as the motorist driving at 30mph on a fast motorway or freeway. For them the risk is uncertain or simply not an element of their cognitions. Similarly, in leadership situations it is possible within some parameters to work out the risk of certain corporate actions; however, in reality, this is not always done, with the effect that what was a risk is turned, perceptually at least, into an uncertainty.

In summary, risk is where we know what is known and we either know what the gaps in our knowledge are (the risk) or that they are reasonably calculable. If we do X, it is likely that Y will happen. If X doesn't happen, Z will. We can to some degree calculate the probability of Y or Z happening.

Uncertainty

Uncertainty, on the other hand, is seen as a situation where the probability of an act cannot be precisely calculated, or at least calculated with an acceptable degree of confidence, for example the chance of catching a particular type of fish in any random spot in the sea on a particular day without any aids like sonar. If we do X, it is possible that Y will happen but we can't be certain. If Y doesn't happen, we don't know what will. Z might happen but equally it might not, and working out what might happen is a guess beyond a risk. Here is an example.

> Bill, a team leader, realizes that two members of his team, Janet and John, aren't performing as they should. Both are arriving at work and meetings late, neither is contributing as much as the rest of the team. Bill has worked with Janet for years and knows that this is unusual behavior. John, on the other hand, is new to the team and to Bill. Bill decides to deal with both Janet and John in the same way. He can predict that Janet will respond positively to the intervention he has planned, while acknowledging that if she doesn't, she is likely to react by getting quieter. Bill weighs up the risk of the possibility of either happening and makes the decision based on that. John, however, is more of an unknown quantity. Bill hopes that John will react positively to the intervention but he is uncertain. John could just as easily react in any other way.

An uncertain situation can either be one where we don't have all the data and therefore can't predict the outcome, or one where we have all the data but when we put it together, the outcome is questionable.

Vagueness

The next step on is any situation where we are not sure what we know about any particular state of affairs and, more importantly, we are not sure what we don't know about the factors that are or might be important in the current scenario. Where there was once clarity and definition, now the thinking, data, and situations lack definition. We can sort of sense or see something but things are not as distinctive and sharply definitive as they were in old world situations. Vagueness is a subproperty of uncertainty and distinct, in that some uncertainties have well-defined elements and gaps in our knowledge, but because of the unique mix of factors, uncertainty is created. Vagueness, on the other hand, is characterized by the lack of definition of the elements. The problem here is that most people will impose a cognitive definition on the situation and find it hard to recognize vague situations, as we only see what we perceive. Further, in an uncertain situation, you may well have clarity in your data and either some data missing, or when you put all the clearly defined data together, you are uncertain as to what it all adds up to. In vague situations, by comparison, the data, situation, and often our thinking lack a discernable shape and clarity. As such, these tend to be conditions where we have little or no idea about the boundaries of our knowledge. So, in addition to being vague about what we know and what matters in any particular situation, importantly, we are also unsure about what we don't know. If we do X, anything could happen.

Vague situations are often referred to as being in or trying to see through a fog, and being able to get through our natural propensity for creating order where there is none (perceptual or cognitive consistency (see Chapter 3) is a skill lacking in many people). Examples of vague situations can be seen during and immediately following a disaster or terrorist incident. As every experienced disaster manager knows, the initial stages of incidents such as the 9/11 World Trade Center attack in New York, the subsea earthquake and resultant Indian Ocean tsunami of 26 December 2004, and the earthquakes that followed the tsunami, and the devastation wrought by hurricane Katrina during August 25–29, 2005, when it made initial land fall near Buras, Louisiana, were all initially vague situations. There is evidence that, immediately before and during the incidents of Katrina, elements of the U.S. government fell into the cognitive consistency trap and failed to see the uncertainty and vagueness inherent in the situation, resulting in a series of inappropriate actions and inactions. Indeed, the vagueness often continues for some considerable time in such situations, but many filter it out. On a less dramatic level, vagueness can be found in companies and organizations around the world, but the systems, policies, and thinking actively sift out the uncertainty and impose order, and, as a result, and this is important, reduce the degrees of freedom they have to act and innovate.

Chaos or total ambiguity

By contrast, chaos or total ambiguity is usually seen as any situation where there is no recognizable data or pattern, no previous experience, and/or no expectation of what might or might not happen, that is, an entirely new situation with no link to any previous situations – in other words, a situation about which there is a large degree of ignorance. It should be noted at this point that ambiguity describes the whole continuum outside certainty, from risk, through uncertainty, vagueness and on to the point of chaos.

Useful for our exploration of ambiguity, the fields of linguistics and some areas of philosophy and logic examine the concept. Ambiguity here is seen as any communication, word, sentence, or phrase that can be reasonably interpreted in more than one way. An example here would be the word "bank", which can mean a type of financial building, turning an aircraft in the air, the sides of a river, the act of putting money or other article in a depository, and other meanings. Ambiguity, linguistically speaking, should not be confused with vagueness, which is where a word or sentence has one meaning but the boundaries are not well defined, for example the words "pile" or the word "bald." The word "pile" has one meaning but working out the distinction between a pile and not a pile is difficult. If you have one sheet of paper, this could not be called a pile of paper. If you had a hundred sheets of paper on top of each other, this would be called a pile. Two sheets of paper would not be called a pile nor probably would three. Similarly, the concept of baldness; the old conundrum "when is a man bald" has a similar property of vagueness about it. We even talk about a man going bald, which suggests that they are not bald at the moment but at some time in the future they will be. So if we remove one hair, will that now make the man bald? Unlikely.

The basis of linguistic and logical ambiguity therefore lies in ascribing more than one meaning to a word, phrase, sentence, and so on. Definitions of logical ambiguity, however, go further and deal with the complexities of human action and thought as well as mathematical ambiguity.

A great example of a complex logical ambiguity, in this case the subset of moral ambiguity, can be seen towards the end of Tolstoy's *War and Peace,* when the two rebel commanders are discussing how they deal with prisoners. If they keep the prisoners, they will be overwhelmed and won't be able to fight. Their dilemma is that to send the prisoners back to the army camp necessitates a long march of many days, with little or no food and water, in appalling weather conditions and across particularly harsh terrain, resulting in much suffering and many deaths. Additionally, it necessitates the use of troops to guard the prisoners on the march, who are then themselves at mortal risk. Few prisoners could ever survive the ordeal.

Denisov sends his prisoners to the army camp knowing that most, if not all, will die. Dolohov, on the other hand, doesn't and argues it is more humane and practical to shoot the prisoners "You send off a hundred prisoners and hardly more than a couple of dozen arrive. The rest either die of starvation or get killed. So isn't it just as well to make short work of them?"

Denisov retorts "That's not the point ... I don't care to have their lives on my conscience. You say they die on the road, well all right. Only it's not my doing."

Which decision you would make would depend on your values and, like Denisov, how they informed your principles. Which decision would you make and how would you rationalize or defend your choice?

Dolohov's decision to kill the prisoners quickly could be seen as a humanitarian choice, in that it prevents suffering, or alternatively it could be seen as a utilitarian choice, in that it saves time and the use and possible elimination of his troops.

Denisov's argument could be seen as humanitarian, in that at least some prisoners should survive, and ethical in that he has not been directly responsible for anyone's death.

As can be seen from this example, once ethical and moral considerations are included, calculating risk or gathering "cold" data does little to help in dealing with ambiguous situations. And yet these are not the only expressions of ambiguity.

The dichotomy of ambiguity

Identification of where you are on the ambiguity continuum, whether you are in a risk, uncertainty, vague, or chaos situation, is most helpful in dealing with problematic sets of circumstances. However, this is easier said than done because in trying to do so we enter into the dichotomy of ambiguity. Simply stated, this is the problem that your perspective of whether you are facing certainty, risk, uncertainty, vagueness, or full-blown ambiguity is subjective and based entirely on your beliefs at the time. It is possible and indeed highly probable that two different people will diagnose where they are on the ambiguity continuum differently. So, for example, a leader who assumes that a situation is the same as a previous one and is in denial, or genuinely can't see any difference between a previous situation and the current one, will take some action based on this understanding of similarity, thinking that there is only a slight risk based on the assumption that they are dealing with the same set of circumstances under the same conditions. But at the other end of the spectrum, another leader might appraise the situation and realize that the conditions have changed so significantly that any previous experience may well not be valid in these circumstances. They believe that they are at best facing a vague situation and that some exploration of the new conditions is likely to yield some useful learning from which to gain additional benefit. That said, attempts at working out where an individual is in relationship to the continuum in any situation will in almost all cases be of great assistance in helping to decide the next course of action, even if this is just to commit to an action or that further open exploration is required. (See Chapters 4–7 for a full description of the different modes of leadership and their relationship to new world thinking.) The difference in how individuals perceive the elements of the ambiguity continuum is linked to their ability to recognize and deal with change, which in turn is determined by the thinking or values system they are using. Recently these have been referred to as vMEMEs.[7] vMEME refers to an adaptation by Beck and Cowan of Richard Dawkin's (*The Selfish Gene*, 1976, Oxford University Press) description of the MEME, which he described as a self-replicating cultural unit of transmission. Unlike genetic evolution, which is transmitted vertically through the generations, the idea of the MEME is the horizontal transmission of cultural norms or ideas. The proposal of the transmission of cultural thinking can be traced back to Plato, with his idea of *eidos*, and through a long line of philosophers, such as John Locke and David Hume, who developed the concepts of "idea" and "perception." The vMEME was created by Beck and Cowan in an attempt to further the idea of the MEME adding values and the attraction of ideas. This in turn is based on the work of Clare Graves in the 1960s. This is part of the basis of spiral dynamics, which in some ways appear to correlate closely with the modes of leadership presented here. However, there is a very good argument that ideas are not "self-replicating" in themselves. Indeed, I would assert that MEMEs are, in fact, lines of logic (paradigms of thinking or approaches to argument) or artifacts that have strong legitimacy in the current context and frequently overturn or replace previous lines of logic that are considered to have less legitimacy in the context. The vMEME or system level of existence that allows the replication of MEMEs can likewise be seen as the development of levels of logic and thought.

The idea of levels of ambiguity

To start to answer the question about why some people, organizations, and countries fair better in changing or continually moving or nonfixed circumstances, or in certain environments or conditions while others collapse requires a thinking shift in itself.

Not only can we discern a continuum of ambiguity from certainty, through risk, uncertainty, and vagueness to chaos or total ambiguity, but as the section above suggests, there are also levels of confidence in each of the five types of ambiguity. Two attributes are necessary and desirable for confidence; the first is the correct identification of the type and nature of ambiguity, and the second is that the individual needs to be comfortable or at least not react with and to any negative emotions that result from being in any type of ambiguity, often for extended periods. Emotional intelligence is hugely important in this aspect. The ability to recognize the emotional effects of an event and ensure that the decisions or actions made are not a result of those emotions often makes the difference in such circumstances. Indeed, leaders who don't recognize an ambiguous situation are often reacting, frequently unconsciously, in a way that moves them from what, to them, are undesirable feelings. This is known as an "away from motivation," which contrasts with "toward motivation," where an individual or group moves toward the attainment of some state.

So what are we to make of these contextual distinctions, which, when compared, appear to say different and often confusing things about ambiguity? While there are similarities and in each context the attributes of the ambiguity appear well defined, the irony cannot be escaped that ambiguity is ascribed a different set of properties in different contexts. The finding that ambiguity can be an ambiguous concept should not be a surprise and certainly does not invalidate the notion, it merely serves to underline the nature of ambiguity and how it lives in many forms. The very nature of the difference between the differing conceptualizations of ambiguity will become a real benefit later when using them to create opportunity and advantage.

The next chapter will explore the varieties of ambiguity, which will lay down the foundations for how great leaders use ambiguity to discover opportunities and take the advantage.

Chronicles of ambiguity

The following narratives will show a series of considerations about ambiguity and further our exploration of the effects, responses, and outcomes of ambiguity in everyday situations. The goal here is not so much to define ambiguity, rather to see what can be learnt about it in order to become outstanding leaders in ambiguous situations.

Would you like the pleasure of my company?

The first scenario is in the context of a boardroom where a number of ambiguous situations arise and a range of responses to them is shown. These exemplify business and work-related ambiguities from the everyday issues of face-to-face conflict to the larger corporate ambiguities that constantly confront organizations and can lead to catastrophic failure.

The boardroom filled up for the meeting. The large wooden table around which all the chairs were situated was complete with bottles of water, glasses, pads of paper, and pencils. Everyone knew his or her place. Briefcases were opened and files of documents, personalized notebooks, laptops, and PDAs started to fill the table. Small groups of people were forming, greetings were exchanged, and general organizational chatter filled the room. The chinking of cups and saucers announced the arrival of the tea, coffee, and biscuits that were being arranged on a side table covered with a white tablecloth. As usual Elaine, the head of HR, was hovering around the table waiting for the catering staff to finish setting out the refreshments. It was not a good idea to distract her at this moment as she closed in for the kill on the chocolate-covered biscuits. Which is precisely why Guy Jefferson, timing his approach to the second, pounced with a beaming smile and a slightly overenthusiastic "Hi Elaine, great to see you," while at the same time offering his right hand. Caught at precisely the moment when she was focused on the four most desirable biscuits on the platter, she had to turn away before securing her prize and face Guy. The fact that her head and eyes lingered for a second on the plate of biscuits as her body moved about amused Guy even more.

"Er, oh hi Guy, er nice to see you."

Elaine now looked nervous and Guy knew it, which only increased his pleasure. She glanced around at the plate.

"Elaine, about this new appraisal system training."

"Er what? Sorry Guy, what about it?"

Forced to shake hands with Guy, her right hand was now even further from the biscuits and not only was he prolonging the handshake but worse, John from finance was heading for the table.

"Can we talk about this after the meeting Guy?" she said, glancing toward John, who was nearly at the biscuits.

Guy saw the look of consternation on her face and the sense of purpose in John's. With a smile and a deft movement, and because he was now facing the refreshments table, he reached past Elaine with his left hand while still holding her right hand and scooped up the four chocolate-covered biscuits. "OK, no problem Elaine, I'll see you later, byeee," Guy said and walked back to the board table with his prize. He knew he couldn't eat them during the meeting, preferring to leave them on the table in full view of Elaine and John, who were now left with a somewhat less appetizing choice. Both their faces looked long. Guy smiled.

Everyone took his or her place.

"Ladies and gentlemen," the chairman, James started. "As we all know, our organization has a long tradition in the sector. We have been market leaders and market beaters for the last 12 years …"

Guy caught the eye of John the marketing director and they both rolled their eyes. John thought, "Here we go again. Another 'in the good old days' pep talk about getting back to traditional values and traditional profits."

Guy was thinking, "It's about time we revisited the retirement age in this company; it's far too high at the moment. Now let me guess, 'We need to get back to basics ...'"

"... but now as you know we are having a problem. We are in a deficit position. What we need to do is get back to basics and ..."

Married to the idea

The second scenario is in the context of two relationships; one is between a wife and husband and the second is between this couple and a couple who are friends of theirs. This account explores and contextualizes interpersonal ambiguities in everyday life.

Janet opened the letters that had just arrived, as she walked back into the dining room. Tony was just finishing his boiled egg.

"This is for you, it appears to be something official," as she handed the brown manila envelope to her husband.

Tony inspected the envelope with his name and address printed on what was clearly a pink preprinted form showing through the clear plastic window.

"Open it then, Tony."

Tony flushed, "I'll take it to work, I'm going to be late."

"Don't be so silly, you have lots of time, open it. I'm curious, it looks quite official."

"Oh it's probably something from the local council."

"Open it then."

Tony ripped the envelope open and peered inside the envelope.

"Oh it's just a work thing; I'll deal with it there."

Janet knew something was wrong. Worried, she said, "Tony what is it? I know you and something is wrong."

"No really darling, it's just a work thing, some admin I have to deal with," he replied weakly.

"Tony, don't lie to me," Janet said sadly. "Something is wrong. You don't live with someone for 17 years and not know when he or she is not telling you the truth. What is it, are you in trouble? Let me see that." She reached across the table to take the envelope.

Tony, looking white now, pulled the letter to him and stared with frightened eyes at his wife. "Please, just let me deal with this. It will be alright," he replied and after a second added, "honestly."

"We will deal with whatever it is, like we deal with everything, together. Now show me the letter Tony," she commanded.

"No," came the simple reply. "Trust me, I need to deal with this," he said, regaining some of his composure.

"What is it Tony, tell me. You are frightening me."

"Honestly, it's just a work thing, please let me deal with it. There is nothing to worry about." He tried to smile at his wife, but she knew he was forcing it.

"Whatever it is, please darling," Janet implored her husband.

"Honestly darling don't worry, just let me deal with it."

"Just tell me what it is." Janet looked directly into Tony's eyes. Tony looked away. "Please."

"Why won't you tell me what it is, Tony?" Janet said firmly.

"Look it's confidential and it's a work thing as I said, so just leave it, OK?" He then got up to leave, taking the letter with him.

Janet got up too and followed her husband into the hall. "Tony, please. What are you hiding?"

"Nothing, just leave it. It's going to be alright, I've got to get to work." And he opened the front door and left.

"Hi Hills, it's Janet."

"Hi Janet, to what do I owe a call at this time of the morning?" Hillary replied down the phone.

Janet explained to her best friend what had happened only minutes before. "I am beside myself with worry. What should I do?"

"I'm not sure. You have absolutely no idea what could be in the letter?"

"No but whatever it was clearly upset Tony. I've never seen him like that before. I am so scared, Hillary. Something is wrong, very wrong."

"OK Jan. I'm sure it's nothing. Maybe it is just a work thing."

"I don't think it was. It's just the way he reacted. I feel it's something else, something bad. I think Tony is in some kind of trouble, Hillary." At that she broke into tears.

"Look Jan, I'll see if John can find something out. They are due to play golf together this afternoon."

"Tony, are you OK?"

"Why do you ask?"

"Jan called Hillary this morning."

Tony's face fell and he looked scared again. "Oh that's what all this is about. Look John, I really don't want to talk about it. It's nobody's business but mine."

"Tony, we have known each other for a very long time. Are you in some kind of trouble? Janet certainly thinks you are and she is very worried."

Talking fast now, Tony replied abruptly, "God, is nothing private any more? I've had enough of this. Look, I'm sorry John, but it's none of your business."

Each of the scenarios above is an example of everyday situations where some form of ambiguity is present. The degree of emotional discomfort in each one is different, as in the perception of the level of ambiguity, and also the amount of cognitive consistency imposed on the situation by each individual.

In the next chapter we will examine the differing types of ambiguity in more detail and the effects these have on people's actions and thoughts.

3 Types of Ambiguity

Trying to encapsulate and define ambiguity is difficult. As noted in Chapter 2, ambiguity is itself ambiguous by its very nature. One reason for this is that the experience of ambiguity is a fairly subjective one and consequently does not affect everyone in the same way. Indeed, in the next chapter, while exploring individual responses to ambiguity, we note that some people are fully aware of a particular ambiguity while others are totally unaware of the existence of that ambiguity. As we have seen in the previous chapter, simply defining and hence recognizing an ambiguity is paradigm-dependent, by which I mean that where an engineer might see uncertainty and a lack of data, a moral philosopher may see a clash of values – the thinking system is different in each case. In this and the following chapter, ambiguity and people's responses to it are explored. Part of that exploration is to examine the structures or lack of structure in a variety of ambiguous situations. The attributes of each of the following types of ambiguity need to be explored:

1 Paradox/contradiction

2 Double bind

3 Chaos/randomness

4 Complexity

5 Dilemmas – moral, ethical, and personal

6 Cognitive and emotional dissonance

Paradox

A paradox is a particular and very interesting type of ambiguity, where two or more things appear to exist at the same time apparently in contradiction with each other, or in a situation that defies commonsense or is counterintuitive. An interesting example of this would be where the following base conditions are seen as being absolutes and true:

- It is wrong to steal.

- Receiving stolen goods is wrong.

- Violence against another human is wrong.

You might find yourself agreeing with all or some of these statements, and yet you might also find yourself siding with Robin Hood who famously robbed the rich to give to the poor.

An important example here is Harvey's Abilene paradox.[1] This particular type of paradox is based on the observation that groups will sometimes act paradoxically, in that the group might end up doing something or act in ways which none of the group find desirable nor would they subscribe to if they had made a choice on their own. The Abilene paradox takes its name from the story Harvey uses to illustrate the phenomenon, based on a family's "groupthink." The story goes like this. During a particularly hot afternoon in Coleman, Texas when the family are relaxing playing dominoes on the porch, the father-in-law suggests that they all take a trip to Abilene, some 53 miles away. The wife agrees that it is "a great idea" and her husband, who does not particularly want to take such a long drive in the heat, agrees. He rationalizes that if everyone else wants to go, it must be him that is "out of step" with everyone else's wishes. So he says, "Sounds good to me, I just hope that your mother wants to go." The mother-in-law, having heard the conversation, also has reservations but answers, "Of course I want to go."

So they duly set off and take the long uncomfortable drive in the heat and dust to Abilene. There they decide to eat at a café where the food is awful and then drive back. Four hours later they arrive back at the house, hot and very uncomfortable. One of them dishonestly says, "that was a great trip wasn't it?", at which point the mother-in-law admits that she would rather have stayed at home but only went along because everyone else had wanted to go. Everyone else then admits to only having agreed because they thought that everyone else wanted to go and the father-in-law finishes the confessions by stating that he didn't really want to go either and that he had only suggested the drive because he thought that everyone else might be bored. The family sit back, perplexed that they had just taken a trip that none of them wanted to take and that they each would have much preferred to have stayed at home relaxing. This type of paradox is a frequently reported characteristic of "groupthink" syndrome.

The paradox of perceptual consistency

Another linked and important paradox in terms of ambiguity, particularly when considering the problems of leadership and organizational development, is the paradox of perceptual consistency, which is connected psychologically to the ideas of cognitive dissonance (discussed later), groupthink, and the subset phenomena of the Abilene paradox.

A famous example of the perceptual consistency paradox was the Japanese attack on Pearl Harbour on December 7, 1941. During the whole period leading up to the attack, the Americans and the Japanese had been engaged in a very public discourse, and on December 8, following the attack, Roosevelt, clearly shocked and wounded by the deception, referred to this in his speech to the nation:

Yesterday, 7 December 1941 – a date which will live in infamy – the United States of America was suddenly and deliberately attacked by naval and air forces of the Empire of Japan. The United States was at peace with that nation and, at the solicitation of Japan, was still in conversation with its Government and its Emperor looking toward the maintenance of peace in the Pacific. Indeed, one hour after Japanese air squadrons had commenced bombing in Oahu, the Japanese Ambassador to the United States and his colleague delivered to the Secretary of State a formal reply to a recent American message. While this reply stated that it seemed useless to continue the existing diplomatic negotiations, it contained no threat or hint of war or armed attack.

When the build-up to the attack was analyzed in retrospect, as is often the case, like the demise of Polaroid examined in Chapter 2, it was found that there were many indicators that things had changed and that a new world existed – a new world in which the signs of war were obvious and the thinking now required was different. In the case of Pearl Harbour, a new world had already dawned and the analysts were busy distorting, deleting, and filtering the data that an attack was about to take place. What should have been a fairly obvious piece of data, which was ignored because it didn't fit with existing thinking, came from one of their own ambassadors who filed a report early in 1941.

On January 27, 1941, Joseph C. Grew, the U.S. ambassador to Japan, wired Washington that he had good information that Japan was planning a surprise attack on Pearl Harbour. Washington did not believe Grew's intelligence; the consensus at the time in U.S. military and political circles was that if an attack came, it would either be in the south, in the Philippines, the direction of Japan's current military expansion against China since 1937, or north into Russia to support Germany. A direct attack on the United States was discounted because it was thought that surprise could not be achieved due to the distances involved. The rationale was that as Japan had expansionist plans and had already attacked and actively annexed large areas of China since 1937, there was every possibility of an attack. Manila was the logical target as it protected the Japanese flank and lines of communication. Anything else just wasn't logical – in their world.

Even more evidence of an attack on Pearl Harbour began to stack up, culminating with some direct evidence from the British, who had broken Japanese naval codes. British intelligence intercepted a message that clearly stated that an attack was imminent and duly passed it on to the Americans. Even direct cipher intelligence from the mouths of the Japanese about their intentions failed to change the paradigm they were using to analyze the situation.

The paradox of perceptual consistency exists whenever anyone, any group, organization, or country, keeps applying the rules of analysis in a context or situation that is substantially different from the one they are actually facing – applying old world thinking to a new world situation. This makes the new world look like the old world through the natural human processes of distorting, generalizing, or deleting data. It is perhaps one of the most common processes of failure when recognizing a new world. Psychological research has shown us that in order to make sense of the world, we need to filter information. If we took in every small piece of data from our surroundings, our brains would quickly become overloaded. In noisy situations, in a night club or industrial situation for example, it is important to be able to filter out what we don't need in order to hear our friend or our child crying above the noise of a playground full of children. Similarly, if I asked you to concentrate on the sensation of your clothes on your body, you should be able to do this, but where were those sensations before I asked you to concentrate on them? The sensations of the touch of your clothes were always there but your mind deleted them as data that was not useful at the time. The mind does what is necessary to allow us to focus on what it thinks we need to. Unfortunately, the very mechanisms that stop us becoming overloaded with superfluous information also blind us to situations when what we perceive is not close enough to a reality that is changing, particularly if we have a strongly invested interest in the old world scenario, as in the example of the Japanese attack on America in 1941.

The paradox of total ambiguity

There are two final paradoxes worth considering here, the paradox of total ambiguity and the paradox of complete certainty.

The former is that point where a situation is so new and so unusual that no previous knowledge or rules apply, where no matter what action you take, an apparently random reaction or even no reaction is the result. And yet at this moment of theoretical total ambiguity, there is for the first time in the journey toward total ambiguity, total certainty – the complete certainty and total knowledge that anything we do is as likely to bring benefit as anything else. Total and pure ambiguity brings with it freedom, the liberty to try anything. Until this point, even though we might not be able to calculate the connection, there must surely be one to discover. The quest before the point of total ambiguity is to explore the terrain to learn the connection that will start the process of reducing the ambiguity back through vagueness, uncertainty, risk, and as close to certainty as is possible – making the new world an old one.

The paradox is that once we have total ambiguity, at the same time we have certainty. Certainty that the situation is ambiguous, that we can do anything and can expect anything to happen. It gives us the certainty to be able to experiment and learn. The more we learn, the less ambiguous the situation gets and the situation moves into vagueness, uncertainty, and finally back to risk and possibly even certainty where we can predict exactly what will happen. At this point, the other side of this paradox comes into play, the paradox of complete certainty. If we ever think that we have total certainty in any action having a particular and predictable effect, then this is the point at which we are most likely to be blind to the next new world, the next paradigm; the point where we get comfortable is the very point we are vulnerable and don't notice subtle changes, where everything appears to be the same – certain.

The double bind

The double bind is a particular type of paradoxical dilemma where two apparently contradictory statements appear to be true at the same time, a sort of damned if you do and damned if you don't scenario. This includes any situation where a person is in receipt of messages, all of which appear to be individually true and yet when put together they contradict each other. Often a double bind gives the appearance of choice where in fact there is none. So a sign that says, "Do not read this sign" is such a case. The most famous double bind is Heller's *Catch 22,* which is the archetypal double bind; you can't leave the army unless you are mad. If you ask to leave, you can't be mad. Only mad people would want to stay in the army and if you want to stay in the army, who are we to argue?

In business there are a number of perceptual double binds that create ambiguity for people and their organizations and frequently have wide-ranging ramifications. For example, the belief that competent women cannot be attractive and that attractive women cannot be competent.[2] Often there are double binds which constrain and control thinking, for example implicit cultural rules within the workplace like "employees who work fourteen hour days and take work home are well thought of," while on the other hand, official memos and policy limit working hours to nine hours a day and forbid work to be taken out of the workplace.

In business a typical double bind is enacted in situations of down-turn. For example, an engineering firm the author was conducting research interviews in posted a large loss for the year. In order to rectify the situation, the board instigated a series of cost-cutting measures, which included a series of redundancies, cutbacks on resources, and the cancellation of new plant which could create joining welds 30 percent faster with 70 percent less errors than the current equipment. The board also stopped all training and develop-ment and then called all departmental heads together to explain the situation. They outlined the cuts to be made, the restructuring plans, and an undisclosed number of redundancies. At the end of the meeting, one of the directors explained that the staff who remained after the cuts would need to find new and innovative products to get them out of the current slump.

The actions of the board created a number of double binds. The first was that just at the moment when the company needed the new equipment to increase quality and speed up production, the appa-ratus became a victim of the cost-cutting exercise. The second double bind created was that just when the company needed a well-trained and competent workforce, with people having to fill in and take on new roles as a result of the redundancies and restructuring, the mech-anism for achieving that through training and development had been dispensed with. Additionally, redundancies are rarely accompanied by a reduction in work, which means that individual workloads increase. Innovation by people in such stressful circumstances is usually difficult at best and at worst impossible, creating another double bind. Often the identification of a double bind alone helps to create conditions of movement out of the ambiguity.

Chaos or randomness

It is possible to find oneself in a situation where there appears to be no discernable patterns from which to predict what might happen next. Examples occur during disaster situations, like 9/11, the 2004 tsunami or hurricane Katrina, or during a war, when people suddenly find themselves in the midst of an incident of such a magnitude that initially they usually report the sense of having nothing to reference what might happen next or make sense of what is happening. The loss of the ability to find normal reference points and the conventional rules, which govern the prediction of what might happen next or what consequences any action or inaction might have initially, creates in many people the sense of a total loss of control, the perception of chaos, and the feeling of anxiety, that random events are happening in which they have no agency nor can they forecast likely futures. All the normal rules that allow prediction of what might follow appear to have broken down. Any action could have, and appears in reality to have, unpredictable consequences. This is where the usual linear logic of cause and effect may exist in theory but breaks down perceptually. We know how something should work but when we try it something else happens. This particular type of ambiguity frequently occurs when trying to predict the behavior of groups or crowds. It is not only natural and human-inspired disasters (such as terrorist attacks) that produce such effects. Traffic accidents, stock market crashes, and customer behavior can all have similar characteristics to chaos. The reality is usually that when viewed from the inside, at first hand and as they happen, such incidents genuinely appear to be chaotic or random. Although analysis after the fact invariably reveals the patterns and suggests what could have been done in such incidents. Two things occur here; first, speed of the events is faster than the rate at which we can discern and learn the patterns prevalent in the situation. Second, there is the cumulative effect of the emotional impact of the sudden change in our surroundings, which overwhelms our cognitive functions, causing us to react out of fear. The response is different for different people, but is invariably automatic and based on reactions to what is perceived to be a life-threatening (either real or imaginary) situation. Two examples serve here.

This first was observed in an organization where it became apparent that one of the senior officers in the organization, who had been employed about six months previously, was not exactly who she had represented herself to be during the recruitment and selection process. Her application claiming to have held a similar senior position in another company was bogus, as were her references, qualifications, and experiences. During the investigation, it was clear that the company concerned had been comprehensively and quite professionally misled, even to the extent that forged degree certificates and other professional qualifications had been used. In addition, the references from her previous company had been forged by a couple of clerks in the other company using company notepaper. Even a phone call to the former company during her recruitment had been intercepted by one of the clerks who acted as the head of department of her former employee and gave a glowing reference, even stating that she was so good in her position that they had offered her promotion to stay and would reemploy her if things didn't work out with the new company. The clerks were receiving ongoing financial reward for their help.

It transpired that the executive officer concerned had in fact only been an administration clerk in her previous company and had managed to fool her new employers for a number of months, although a couple of other senior managers had suspected something was wrong when she would not make any decision without having to consider the matter in her office alone first. Once suspicion was raised and her emails examined, it transpired that she was communicating with others outside the organization (some of whom she was in the process of recruiting into the company), passing them details of the day-to-day workings, personalities, issues, and financial accounts of the company in question. Using her external network, she would then concoct a plausible response or decision and communicate it inside.

Two things happened when she was exposed that are exemplars of the types of response under consideration here. The person under investigation reacted violently to the allegations, angrily accusing her accusers of fraudulent and malicious prosecution and threatening physical violence, to the extent that security had to be called to ensure the safety of the other employees. She also began a process of producing ever more ludicrous forgeries to back her story up, printouts from bogus websites, and further forged documentation from previous companies. She then started a lengthy legal action against her new employer that eventually collapsed, but not after a considerable time and cost to the company.

The second thing that happened was that once it became known what had happened, a number of other senior officers in the company, who had either been duped by the fraudulent executive officer or had been part of the recruitment process, started a robust defense of her. While this didn't last very long once the overwhelming nature of the evidence against her became known, it did cause severe problems at the most senior level in the company for some considerable time, and diverted the energies of a significant number of senior members away from their more constructive corporate tasks, to the extent that production and employee issues arose later as a direct result. The estimated direct and indirect cost of the incident and subsequent production and staffing issues was calculated to be hundreds of thousands of pounds, with the fallout directly caused by the often emotionally driven reactions of many of the individuals as the episode unfolded, accounting for a substantial proportion of the final figure.

The second example comes from the author's direct experience of training disaster management trainers at the Resilience Centre at Cranfield University and around the world for a variety of governments. An important part of such training is to equip the students with the ability to recognize and deal with the emotional impact that a disaster or terrorist incident has on an individual and how it affects their decision-making abilities. An evaluation of such training showed that disaster managers had been fully equipped with and were knowledgeable about the models of how best to plan for and deal with disasters, how to manage disaster response centers, construct post-incident logistical processes, casualty handling, and the many other tasks that are required following a major incident.

When case studies of real-life incidents were examined, however, it transpired that little of the learning was being put into effect during incidents. Stories abound of disaster managers creating slow and bureaucratic systems which hampered relief efforts, trained operators seizing up under the horror of what surrounded them (in one major global incident, the relief commander broke down and lapsed into total inaction and refused to make any decisions in case more lives were lost), counterproductive decisions being made, and physical fights breaking out between rescuers. This is not to suggest that this is always the case because it isn't, however, there is a wealth of evidence to show that following a significant proportion of disasters, lives have been lost due to poor disaster management, a lack of creative problem solving, and slow or misguided decision making due mainly to disaster managers' emotional responses to the apparent chaotic and random nature of the disaster.

The aim of such training now is to augment the models, the development of standing operating procedures and theory, with the disaster managers' ability to be able to deal effectively with their own and others' emotional responses. Additionally, to be able to creatively solve problems there and then in chaotic and disconnected (random) situations. A key ability of a disaster manager is to be able to start in a situation where there is little or no knowledge, quickly formulate a plan of action that will frequently not be the same as previously formulated, published plans, recognize new data and the consequences of them as they arrive, and change the plan accordingly, as the validity and reliability of the data increases. Professor Ian Davis, a close friend and advisor to the British government on disaster management, holds that creativity and flexibility are the hallmarks of a good disaster manager. Similarly, great leaders can comfortably operate in times when ambiguity abounds and lead people through what appear to be random and chaotic times, which are so uncomfortable to others that they seize up or find it hard to perform. Emotional intelligence is a key factor in dealing with ambiguity, particularly those situations close to chaos where little or no knowledge or experience is available.

Complexity

Complexity can be defined as a state somewhere between orderliness and chaos or randomness. It is a state where there is variation without being totally chaotic and completely unpredictable, a place where predicting outcomes has a range of complexity and, by definition, difficulty. The more complex a situation, the harder and more time-consuming it is to predict the outcome or solve a problem. While many disciplines have constructed their own definitions of complexity, there is currently a move to treat complexity as a subject in itself in order to examine phenomena that previously had to be simplified and modeled. This previous difficulty in understanding the complexity of things such as anthills, the brain, traffic flows, group behavior, or stock markets, for example, was in part caused by our natural propensity for "seeing" simple patterns thus masking the complexity.

In essence, complexity encompasses nature in that, unlike the pattern finding we usually engage in when trying to solve problems or make decisions, there may not be fixed relationships between variables or fixed behaviors, or even fixed qualities or quantities, which means that it is entirely possible that a function in a system is undefined or not yet identified. While this may appear to be a tenuous and abstract concept, such systems form the majority of our world where there is no one-to-one direct correlation between factors, for example living organisms, inorganic natural systems such as rivers and clouds, and social systems like organizations, market dynamics, and customer behavior.

The most frequent responses of a leader to a complex situation (where relationships between the factors observed are not fixed so that they do not always act the same way, or that behaviors vary, or that the amount or qualities experienced changes in some unknown way) is either to impose or imagine a false order or to ignore or simplify the variance. For example, you might know, say, 23 people, some friends and some work colleagues. You might be able to predict how each of them might react to a certain situation. Of some of the 23 people, you would be able to say with confidence that your prediction will be relatively accurate, because their response is less likely to vary; however, with others, your confidence about how they might respond may be low, because they are less predicable in their behavior. This is not just a function about how well you know each individual. Some people you know will be more predicable in the way they behave with others, and some people you know the only thing you can predict is that they could do anything!

Now imagine putting all 23 people into the same space and asking them as a group to find the solution to a problem that you are currently working on and trying to predict what would happen; how they each react, individually and to each other, and how long it takes them to reach a solution – now you have complexity. The mixture of 23 different people trying to work as a group would produce a feeling and a system of working that would be unique to any other group of people – this group would have an emergent identity and properties that are more than the sum of the individuals involved.

Complexity can appear, especially initially, to be chaotic or random situations, however, there are discernable patterns to be discovered which can help the leader. The main point here is that complexity is *not* a synonym for complicated, rather it is seen as a system or process of interconnected parts or factors which interact together to form an emergent property which is more than and different from the sum of the parts.

Complexity in organizations has a number of properties worth considering here. To a leader without an understanding of complexity, these attributes can appear to all but the most generative leaders to be chaotic and it is unlikely that leaders of any mode except mode four (see Chapter 7) will be able to utilize this complexity profitably. Additionally, it is unlikely that leaders with a low tolerance for ambiguity will be able to recognize the value of complexity in organizational settings, and they are likely to react to a complex situation by trying to control it and shut down the attributes which lead to the all-important and useful emergent properties that complex situations deliver. The following is a brief summary of the attributes of complex systems[3] that good leaders should be able to identify and use to create emergent advantages, particularly in organizational and market contexts:

■ *Connectivity profile*: The individuals or parts involved have an eclectic range of information or inputs and a similar number of outputs or outcomes. This is known as a fan-in/fan-out arrangement. In an organizational structure, for example, it is usual to find that the system has more than one source and type of information using a number of different paradigms. Likewise, the outcomes will be disseminated to more than one source. The individuals or parts have multiple loyalties and connections to affect the desired results. It is the diverse and extensive nature of the connections available to the system that underlies its flexibility, farsightedness, and quality of analysis.

■ *Transition exponent*: It is usual in complex systems that the number of inputs and outputs are roughly equal. If there are more inputs than outputs, the system tends toward a static or paralyzed situation rather than an emergent one, and if the outputs exceed the inputs, a chaotic or fluctuating situation often arises.

■ *Learning availability*: A hugely important aspect of complexity and leadership is that each of the parts or individuals have the ability to learn from their experiences and, importantly, at any time to change the rules they are applying to ensure pragmatic and accomplished solutions, if necessary breaking the rules and making new ones to achieve the desired outcome or transitions. A key component of learning availability within complex systems is the ability not to become trapped by previous learning, recognizing contextually obsolete learning, and moving beyond it to create new paradigms. (See the following section for a fuller discussion about learning and the nature of knowledge.)

■ *Operational parallelism:* This is often a hard attribute for managers and most leaders to accept in a complex system, however, the world's best universities operate on this principle where each member acts largely autonomously and in parallel, rather than being organized in series like a production line. The emergent property of parallelism is that the system adapts quickly to new world scenarios and usually in completely unexpected ways. There is an emergent creativity and adaptability that occurs in complex systems because of this.

■ *Interaction variability:* The parts or individuals will change and rechange who they interact with and also how they interact to ensure that the data comes from and goes to the places they are needed most – to ensure the highest learning availability. This is a flexible element of the individual's interconnectivity profile. They will forge, change, and drop relationships dependent on efficacy.

■ *Feedback loops:* Complex systems will have a series of feedback loops, whereby the learning achieved is constantly fed back to where it is needed for constant improvement. The system is usually always on the move and dynamic (see the notes below about the types of complexity). It should be noted, however, that feedback loops are not set out in advance, planned or forced, nor are they defined beforehand. They happen based on the principle of efficacy.

■ *Control ability:* There is an element of control in complex systems, which prevents explosive runaway processes and totally chaotic tendencies. The control ability in a complex system does not control the system as such, rather it is more like a flexible set of guiding principles that guide the path of the individuals while allowing for freedom of movement and the ability to change the principles.

■ *External boundaries:* Linked to the control ability, the nature of external boundaries in a complex organization is somewhat like a flexible and dynamic tube or wrapper that maintains an energetic and forward orientation while allowing exploration and expansion of the periphery. It can be seen as more of a check to allow development, evolution, and self-organizing freedom without the system becoming overly volatile and unstable. The boundaries are neither open nor closed. Closed boundaries promote stagnation and convergent thinking, while fully open boundaries can cause runaway processes and panic in those who need structure.

■ *Strategic basins of attraction:*[4] These allow for multiple ways and methods of achieving the same goal by gathering together in the same basin all the networks or communities of practice that have a positive stake in the system and its goals. Any of the networks that become redundant or fail are removed from the basin and any new networks that offer an advantage are included. By now you will have noticed that loyalty does not really have a place in a complex system except to that of learning. People, relationships, ideas, networks, and so on are all expendable if their usefulness wanes.

■ *System function:* In any situation of complexity, there are usually multiple realities, goals, communication processes, and functions. These provide considerable resilience and multidimensional capability, but are hard for all but generative individuals to cope with and use to their advantage.

■ *Holographic building blocks:* In any complex system, a whole series of interconnecting subsystems can be discerned that give a modular and fractal structure, and at the same time each subsystem is autonomous and reflects the higher purposes of the whole. In an organization these might be seen as independent groups that might appear to be maverick to some, but on closer scrutiny actually serve and reflect the aims of the organization, albeit in a diverse form. A lack of discernment of the holographic attributes in diversity is the most frequent cause of "oddballs" being sidelined and undiverse practice.

■ *Emergent properties:* One of the most significant attributes of complexity is the phenomenon of emergent properties. These could be functions or outputs that materialize by themselves and are self-organizing; they have not been planned or imposed. It is the leaders' ability to see and seize such emergent properties and profit from them that is often the key to turning ambiguous situations to their advantage, where others are overwhelmed by the complexity confronting them. Emergent properties are what generative leaders try to generate and seize the advantage from. These are the true advantages of complexity.

■ *System resilience:* A key component in any complexity, this is the ability to handle *change* positively. It is worth noting here that there is a difference between redundancy and resilience. Redundancy is a position where there are fail-safe structures, in complexity it is possible that things work too well and resilience is lost.

An example from World War II serves here. During Germany's attack on Russia in Operation Barbarossa, the superior and perfectly machined weaponry of the Third Reich initially gave them the advantage over the almost thrown together, rudimentary weapons of the Russians. Until winter came, that is, when the Germans found that their beautifully engineered rifles and guns started to seize up as the metal contracted. The more elementary guns of the Russians, while less accurate, proved resilient in the temperatures encountered during the winter of 1941.

Another somewhat sobering and more contemporary example of system resilience can be seen in the discovery that some microbes known as "psychrophiles" (lovers of ice) can live in frozen conditions of up to −20°C for hundreds of thousands, if not millions, of years anywhere up to four kilometers deep in solid ice.[5] Psychrophiles (living fungi, bacteria, viruses, and yeasts) up to 400,000 years old have been found in Antarctic ice and millions of years old in permafrost. The question is, what happens when the ice melts and releases the psychrophiles? Scientists are currently concerned that global warming could release viruses for which we have long lost resistance to. The microbes have resilience without redundancy.

■ *Distributed control:* This is one of the fundamental principles of generative leadership (Chapter 7), where control and power is distributed throughout the system. This is the defining characteristic that most leaders find difficult, the distribution of control and power. In complex systems, control and power sit where they are most effective, not just with the leader. Distributed control works on the principle of expertise leading while getting constant feedback and challenge to keep the expertise fit. In such circumstances, generative leaders concede leadership to those most suited to it in any context, whereas most other leaders will maintain control.

■ *Information flow:* In a complex system, information works like a social structure, without predefined channels. The flow is efficient and effective, skipping blocks and restrictions if necessary. It should be noted that in a complex system informational efficiency finds its own levels of quantity. Overload is usually a sign of overengineering or control. In a truly complex system, increasing information flows can denote a move toward chaos from stability, while most complex systems move between not quite stable to not quite chaotic. Information flow is based on scaleable network theory.[6]

■ *Output variability:* Little variability in output such as production or sales usually suggests a tendency toward stability, but with it comes stagnation, little innovation, and decreased opportunities. Conversely, high variability implies a move toward chaos and high ambiguity. A move in this direction increases creativity, innovation, and opportunity but is frightening for many individuals, leaders, groups, and organizations. However, it is when outputs are variable that new products and opportunities emerge.

While not all the above properties need to be present for complexity to exist, the vast majority of them will be identifiable in any given situation where it has been allowed to emerge. Most leaders are likely to see only chaos and will rarely notice the profitable emergent properties and inherent creativity of the situation. If such leaders are put into or take over a complexity situation, they will usually react to their own feelings of discomfort brought on by a sense of a lack of control or a fear that if they don't manage the situation, anything could happen. Anything happening for a generative leader (for a full description of each mode of leadership, see Table 1 in Part II) is a different experience than for other leaders. The generative leader, who not only likes complex situations, but also actively creates them, will see anything happening as a world of unknown possibilities, in which anything could be the next big idea or product. Technical leaders (see Chapter 4) have a fear that if anything can happen, when it does happen, it will be negative. Cooperative leaders (Chapter 5) see the possibility of anything happening as a distraction. They usually have a fixed idea of the outcome they want and have worked out how to get it. Anything happening, especially if there are multiple and often parallel "anything happenings," will be seen as an interruption to their goals. Collaborative leaders (Chapter 6), on the other hand, are usually excited by the prospect of something new happening, but it needs to be within certain parameters and with not too many happening at the same time. These are busy people who need to have everything agreed and "bought into" by the team. Lots of emerging new ideas and properties of any situation are truly welcomed and what they want in theory, however, in reality, the problem they face is that the system they use to try to deal with it is hardly functional. Sets of complicated communication networks and an abundance of time is required to ensure that there is a consensus about everything that is happening, which means that consensual leaders and their teams quickly become swamped and overworked. Mode four or generative leaders, on the other hand, don't try to control, do not have a singular goal, nor are they interested in a consensus, indeed, diversity of approach and arguments are seen as a positive by these individuals. They are truly open to whatever emerges from the complexity, in addition to the goals they have. In short, they are inveterate learners, and they treat and understand knowledge differently from other people. They will catch and explore the possibilities of anything and everything they notice. The emergent properties of complexity are the foundations, for the generative leader, of constant and continual learning, innovation, and the creation of new worlds, futures, and possibilities.

The complexity of knowledge – it's not a fact

As noted above, generative leaders treat knowledge as part of the complexity they naturally notice and strive for in the world around them. They understand and use knowledge in a different way from many others.

Often when we talk about knowledge, knowing something, or we make a proclamation about "getting the facts," or "knowing the facts," we are making a series of assumptions about the character of knowledge and thus the nature of learning.

For example, there are a whole set of attributes that many connect to the thought of going to a university or school, or taking an exam. This usually goes along the lines of being taught new knowledge; studying or learning is often synonymous with committing to memory material that has been taught so that the student can regurgitate the facts later in an exam. Many MBAs and other qualifications are founded on the ideal that the student will go to an institute where a lecturer will teach and the student will learn what has been taught. Additionally, teachers often talk about the primary role of the activity of teaching as the transmission of knowledge. Calling someone a teacher or lecturer presupposes that the teacher knows something and that the student needs to know what the teacher has to impart, and that the act of transmission is a simple process of lecturing. The teacher talks, shows pictures, diagrams, television or video/DVD clips and the student learns in a direct one-to-one way. This is known as the banking theory of learning. The model goes something like this.

The person with the currency (the teacher) goes to a bank and hands over a certain amount of cash. The teller (the student) takes the cash and puts it in a safe (his or her memory). When the person, (the teacher) comes back to withdraw their money (an exam), the teller (the student) goes back to the safe, takes out the money and gives exactly the same amount back, with the addition of a little extra interest.

This analogy lies behind the philosophy of many teachers and students about the nature of knowledge and what schools and universities are there for. Indeed, many large organizations have set up their own corporate universities built on the same principles, usually surrounding the ideals of transmitting best practice (as knowledge). This all makes for certain assumptions about the nature of knowledge, for example that the knowledge is right, that is, that it is a fact, and that as a fact, it is proven. Knowledge or facts are therefore seen as stable, it was right in the past, it is right now and it will be right in the future. So, knowledge can be easily "transmitted," like the banking analogy above, and once you "know the facts," you can then do things with them like solve problems.

If only it were so simple. The problems with such an impoverished view of knowledge and learning are that it gives the job of creating knowledge to someone else, creates dependency, and the stagnation of wisdom. Knowledge is always learnt rather than created and discovered. In this paradigm, a fact is unassailable (true) and unquestionable. Mode one, two and three leaders all treat knowledge in such a way, they have an implicit faith that knowledge is static. Their currency is knowing facts, and with facts, problems can be solved. There is little awareness that facts are dynamic.

Generative leaders (mode four) appreciate that knowledge is a dynamic concept; knowledge changes, grows, and becomes outdated. In effect, they implicitly understand that all knowledge is a *current* line of reasoning. Any fact might work right now and make perfect sense, given the current system of thinking (paradigm), but change the circumstances or the system of thinking and the old knowledge falters. Facts are contextual and arguable.

Thinking differently, questioning the current perceived wisdom, and looking at the evidence in different ways can frequently identify a new world. The following is a good example.

It concerns the discovery of plate tectonics by the German meteorologist Alfred Wegener,[7] who proposed the geological theory of "continental drift" in 1912. This flew in the face of the then current theories that explained the earth's physical geography. The conventional wisdom of the dominant group (COWDUNG)[8] in the early 1900s was that the earth's major geographical features were formed by the cooling and contraction of the earth. So critical was the reaction to Wegener's theory that other geographers would wait in the lecture theatre until Wegener started to teach his students and would then walk out of his lecture en masse in protest at his mad arguments. Not only did the criticism come from his peers in the meteorological and geographical sciences, but also from academics in other disciplines. W.B. Scott, former president of the American

Philosophical Society, even called the theory of continental drift "utter damned rot."[9] Another scientist stated, "If we are to believe [this] hypothesis, we must forget everything we have learned in the last 70 years and start all over again," and a British geologist at the time said that "anyone who valued his reputation for scientific sanity ... would never dare support such a theory."[10]

The aim of this example is to show the dynamic nature of knowledge. Indeed, while the general paradigm that Wegener proposed is still currently and generally agreed, the mechanism he proposed by which huge geographical plates move has since been disproved and updated. The point is that knowledge grows, develops, and is refined and even changes under different conditions. William Perry,[11] an epistemologist, views all knowledge and facts as an argument. Arguments differ from opinions as they are based on evidence. Good evidence is both as valid and reliable as possible. The validity and reliability of any data is based on the context at a time. Additionally, we never know at any time exactly what evidence is fundamental to the argument, we can only discover this through further exploration. The upshot of all this is that knowledge is itself an example of complexity and the facts of one context can never be fully relied on in another. History is littered with paradigm shifts, where the facts and accepted wisdom have to change in the light of new world conditions. One example from neurology shows how the conventional wisdom of science changes and the old world thinking is exposed as a restricting and dogmatic system of thinking rather than the fact-based knowledge it once was perceived as being.

Before 2005, it was well understood that neurons (nerve cells) only produced one type of neurotransmitter. However, in 2005 it was found that this might not be accurate. Neurons in the brain can be either excitatory, sending a signal that stimulates cells to do something, or inhibitory, telling cells to stop doing what they're doing. Disturbances in the inhibitory system contribute to disorders such as epilepsy and have been linked by some researchers to schizophrenia.

Neurotransmitters (chemicals by which the nerve cells communicate) have until recently been categorized the same way, either as excitatory or inhibitory. As such, scientists believed that excitatory neurons only release excitatory neurotransmitters, such as glutamate, and inhibitory neurons release only inhibitory neurotransmitters, such as GABA or glycine.

This is what everyone thought until 2005, when a postdoctoral researcher called Deda Gillespie was taking measurements of an inhibitory neuron in some brain tissue from a rat. Gillespie found that it was emitting excitatory glutamate, which was previously understood only to be an inhibitory transmitter. At first it was thought that there was a problem with the experiment, however, after consistent checking and double-checking, it was found that the result was unbelievably correct – this was excitatory glutamate, which went against the then current scientific facts. Others have repeated the findings and there is now a race on to find out why this is happening and what it means now that the old facts have been usurped.

With the old system of thinking replaced, Karl Kandler, another neurologist from the University of Pittsburgh, noted, "Once a dogma is broken, then people start looking for it in their systems."

And the new world thinking becomes the new conventional wisdom that is waiting to be overthrown.

For each age is a dream that is dying,
Or one that is coming to birth.

Knowledge and facts are as dynamic as the world around us.

Dilemmas – moral, ethical, and personal

Another form of ambiguity is created when people feel that they are in a dilemma. A dilemma usually involves a conflict between two or more competing values within the same person or system.

For example, in Book I of Plato's *Republic*, Cephalus defines "justice" as speaking the truth and paying one's debts. Socrates disagrees and states that it would be wrong to repay certain debts, for example to return a borrowed weapon to a friend who was currently suicidal. Plato is not arguing that repaying a debt is not a moral issue but showing that where differing moral beliefs come into conflict, a decision needs to be made as to which one takes priority.

In this case, Socrates argues that protecting life has priority over the moral responsibility to repay a debt.

The feature of any dilemma is conflict. In this case, there is a conflict between two moral obligations. While in Plato's case it is a fairly easy choice, others are harder, for example the dilemma faced by many whistleblowers, and indeed those who decide not to "blow the whistle" still make such a decision. What would you do if you discovered that your organization was making profit illegally but that if you made the irregularities public you were certain that the company would cease trading and a lot of people would lose their jobs?

Such dilemmas can cause uncertainty and ambiguity for those who experience them and those on the receiving end of the final decision. An understanding of the different thinking options and how they each approach such problems will help to unravel dilemmas (see Part II).

Cognitive dissonance

In 1956, the psychologist Leon Festinger proposed what became known as the theory of "cognitive consistency," out of which came the idea of "cognitive dissonance."[12] Basically, the idea is that the way we see the world at any time is based on and filtered by cognitions. Cognitions are attitudes, values, beliefs, emotions, and goals that come together and form a perspective. For example, a person who is racist or sexist will have a collection of values, beliefs, attitudes, and emotions about people of a difference race or gender that, when they are dealing with such people, will give them a particular viewpoint that will usually make them interpret the actions of people of a different race or gender more negatively than they would do with anyone else. A racist's cognitions – the amalgam of their values, beliefs, attitudes, emotions, and goals – create filters, distortions, deletions, and generalizations about people of the target race. Festinger's theory is that we look for and try to create cognitive consistency, in other words, we often make the facts fit the world we expect. This not only happens with prejudices, but every day we filter, delete, distort, and generalize information because of the wish for continuity and stability in the world – we create cognitive consistency.

Cognitive dissonance refers to those times when two or more

competing cognitions are held simultaneously, creating a conflict that cannot easily be made consistent in the mind of the individual. For example, a sexist who believes that women are bad drivers and is beaten by a woman who then goes on to win a driving competition is likely to suffer cognitive dissonance. In effect, cognitive dissonance occurs when an individual has to make a choice between conflicting attitudes, values, beliefs, or emotions. People deal with cognitive dissonance in different ways depending on the level of threat the dissonance poses to the individual's beliefs and self-identity or the level of discomfort the dissonance creates within the individual, which is based on the thinking system employed.

The example Festinger uses is a person who enjoys smoking and is told by a doctor just what harm it is doing to them. This sets up a cognitive dissonance that can be alleviated in a number of ways. First, they could give the health cognitions higher importance and stop smoking. They could equally give the pleasure cognitions greater importance and decide that "one could live a long life in misery or a short one happily." Alternatively, they could boost the importance of the smoking cognitions by convincing themselves that they need to smoke to be able to concentrate, or not gain weight, or relax. On the other hand, they might seek to reduce the health cognitions by telling themselves that in the scheme of things, the danger posed by smoking is negligible in comparison to the danger of death or injury in a car accident. Finally, they could deny that one of the cognitions even exists, completely writing out what the doctor said, for example even to the extent that they totally "forget" the visit and will deny that they ever spoke to the doctor. This latter option (usually unconscious) is far more common than might at first be expected, to the extent that some people actually don't see something that is physically in front of them, so great is the dissonance for that individual.

In 1999, Daniel Simons and Christopher Chabris, psychologists at the University of Illinois, surprised the scientific community with a series of visual cognition experiments which showed that people don't see things that physically exist and are very visible, if they don't expect to see the object.[13] In the experiment, people were asked to watch a video of a group of students bouncing basketballs. The viewers were asked to count the number of times one team bounced the basketballs. While they were watching, a person dressed as a gorilla slowly wove their way through the group, faced the camera, waved at the viewers, and walked slowly off screen. More than 60 percent of viewers failed to notice the gorilla.

This and a further series of experiments graphically display how cognitive dissonance, which is created by the need for cognitive consistency, can result in the total deletion in the minds of individuals and groups of even the most obvious and observable phenomena. This then explains why some leaders are blind to changing events and new worlds. Those who do perceive change and notice conflicting events will consciously have to endure the uncomfortable experience of dissonance, or ambiguity. Those with the highest tolerance to ambiguity are less likely to suffer the delusional effects of cognitive consistency, but will have to bear the discomfort created by the conflicts that the interaction between our cognitions and reality presents. Those with ready, common wisdom and common-sense explanations of new world events may just be the victims of their own minds and their own emotions striving for consistency. Those who recognize the conflicts inherent in a new world versus old world situation will have to endure the discomfort of the dissonance to allow the emergent properties of the new world to materialize. The perception of ambiguity is a state created by cognitive dissonance, which itself is a reaction to our need for cognitive consistency in the face of world conditions as we start to realize that our internal representation of the world doesn't match the reality anymore.

Part II
The Nature of Leadership

People are disturbed, not by things, but by the views they take of them. Epictetus, Greek Stoic philosopher (c.55–c.135)

The following chapters explore leadership in situations of ambiguity, arguing that the leaders' responses to ambiguity are one of the most critical factors for successful leadership outcomes, both for the leader, others affected by them, and the organization. Chapters 4–7 review the research evidence about effective leadership and the factors that contribute to superior performance in ambiguous contexts. This part of the book explores the rise and fall of formal leaders through hierarchical promotions or direct employment, and the rise of "informal" leaders whose influence and ability to deal with ambiguity makes them powerful without the hierarchical structure. Leadership here is seen as an activity rather than a set of personality characteristics.

During research at Cranfield on leaders' responses to ambiguity and the environments they engender, the author interviewed and observed formal hierarchical and informal leaders and members of their teams in a number of organizations around the world. These include a number of universities, police forces, health, defense and security agencies, a merchant banking corporation, a heavy engineering firm, and a transport company in the UK, Malaysia, the Philippines, Kenya, New Zealand, Singapore, and South Africa. In research published in 2003, it was found that leaders usually claimed that their work involved the honorable leadership activities of working on strategy, developing vision and values, and leading their team step by step through the strategy toward the goals.[1] The reality, however, was that the interviewed leaders were almost wholly engaged in "micro-management," supervision, and administrative duties.

The author's research did show only a few exceptions to this and

Table 1 The four leadership modes

Mode	1	2
Activity	Technical	Cooperative
Vision	Leader defines	Multiple (individual) visions
Power	Leader	Split/individuals
Characteristics	Certainty/safety, high risk for leader	High risk for every individual, scary for some, invigorating for others
Responsibility	Ascribed to leader or leader takes	No one individual
Risk	Risks ignored/reduced as much as possible	Risks minimized
Orientation	Fact based/dualism/definite answers	Opinion-based/multiplicity/multiple/subjective realities
Problem type	Type I problems Technical problems that require technical solutions	Type II problems Cooperative problems that require cooperative solutions
Problem solving	Standardized problem-solving methods/imposition of leader's solutions	Research-based problem solving based on the "facts"
Values	Leader's values	Mixed values
Ambiguity	Little to no ambiguity/all ambiguity reduced	Internal ambiguity/conflict – seeks to reduce external ambiguity
Reactions to uncertainty	Either not recognized, displacement behavior, denial or aversion	Ambiguity keenly felt. Immediate steps taken to reduce ambiguity
They say	"Others say" "The facts are"	"I think" "I know"
Diversity	Diversity not tolerated/similarity encouraged/enforced	All equal/diversity tolerated within bounds

3	4
Collaborative	Generative
Single shared vision/consensus	Expert views explored and built on
Group/collective	Leader and experts – the flexible team
Supportive/equality, low risk for individuals, high risk for collective	Explorative, generative and innovative. Risks welcomed and explored
Shared/everyone	Everyone shoulders the responsibility for everything
Risks explored that bring about equal opportunities	Risks enjoyed and explored for opportunities
Argument based on evidence/constructivism/uncertainty/ambiguity	Creative divergent and evidence-based convergent thinking
Type III Problems that require adaptive responses and solutions	Type IV Generative problems that require future pacing and a creationist paradigm
Adaptive creative thinking processes	Creative/innovative non-problem-solving approach – generative
Consensus/shared values	Values worked out to suit situation context
All ambiguity explored and embraced for learning – lots of talk, not much action	All ambiguity explored for learning and opportunities – action taken
Quite happy to remain in ambiguous situations for extended periods	Seek out ambiguity to find the advantage
"I'm not sure" "At the moment we think"	"I don't know" "At the moment I think" "I wonder if?" "Let's try" "Let's act"
Diversity of thinking/talent/perspectives is accepted deep down. We are all equal	Diversity is essential. Try to get as many divergent perspectives as possible

analysis of the interviews and direct observations of day-to-day activities suggested that there were broadly four modes of leadership, which corresponded to four different types of work environment and responses to ambiguity.

Table 1 provides a summary of the modes of leadership and the research findings.

Mode One: Technical Leadership

4

In essence we have become addicted to the certainty, sureness, or sense of security that our faith provides. **Reverend Leo Booth, English rector, author and theologian (1946–)**

The largest discrepancy between leadership talk and actual practice was found in what is labeled mode one technical leadership scenarios. Their view of leadership is that they are in charge, they have the knowledge and ability to use it and their subordinates (their language) do not. As a specific strategy, most mode one leaders said they actively kept information to themselves and away from other people in their domain, in the belief that only they have the overview necessary to make the decisions.

An exemplary illustration of this mode was found in a group I was working with a few years ago. Having been brought in by the leader to facilitate a "team-building" process, it was quickly found that the group was under official scrutiny due to performance issues and "informal" complaints of mismanagement. It transpired that the leader had not informed anyone in the department concerned that they were under review. Some people in the department accidentally "discovered" the situation in conversations outside the group. The leader's defense was that he was there to protect his people from the uncertainty of such a destructive process, which he knew was quite likely to result in the department being split up and subsumed in other departments. This leader stated that he was certain they would survive as a unit, with just a few of the poorer performers being removed. As it transpired, he was removed by the board.

Such a command and control ideology is typical of technical leadership.

Another example of the behavior of a mode one leadership scenario comes from a group meeting I was asked to observe by the leader as an example of successful leadership.

There was no denying that the group concerned did have a fairly high income generation ability with the company. I was also to discover that this was down to two unusually gifted individuals, one of whom was the leader, and that the group's staff turnover ran at about 90 percent per two years. During the meeting, a discussion started about the best method of making sales contacts in a particular company. The discussion was interesting in that the only ideas tabled came from the leader, with everyone else either agreeing or abstaining, making no contribution at all. During the "discussion," a new member of staff suggested a different approach. The manager, who was also always the chair, smiled and stated that he (the new member of staff) had not been in the company long enough to know what to do. The leader ended by saying publicly, "this is not a democracy, it's a dictatorship and I am the dictator."

During the research, the opportunity arose to observe a job selection process in a department whose head had been identified as a mode one leader.

Following the interviews, there was a long discussion about which candidate would fit in. This turned out to be a deciding factor even in the face of a better qualified and experienced candidate; the "fit" test logic is frequently used in mode one groups. For example, I observed one mode one group doing individual presentations about their views of where the department should go next. Amazingly, seven of the presentations were almost identical, while only one was different. As the woman presented her vision, I noticed a number of people in the group who had their legs crossed also had their feet wagging. The presentation was met by silence and facial expressions that suggested disapproval. At the end of her talk, the leader sat forward and said, "Well, as ever, a different view from Elaine. I don't think that we need to go into it too far. Thank you Elaine. Someone else?"

These incidents give a clue as to how mode one leaders and their groups deal with ambiguity and diversity. Within mode one groups, few deviations from the norm are acceptable. Interestingly, there are a number of reactions to ambiguous situations apparent with mode one leaders, and these are now discussed.

Mode one reactions to ambiguity 1: There is only certainty

The first response to ambiguity was found by accident during a fact-finding process with a group of managers who were about to undergo a training program prior to a merger of departments.

During the preliminary analysis sessions, two of the managers insisted that the merger was a ruse for some unfathomable management purpose. No amount of explanation, visits from senior management or even being shown the business plan could shake their belief that the merger was not about to happen. This belief continued even in the face of all the signs of an imminent merger, like plans for new office spaces, a visit by the transport company who were to move the office equipment, and innumerable meetings about the situation.

When questioned further, both managers stated categorically that there was no uncertainty in their lives, not just in their jobs but in their lives. Thus began the uncovering of a small group of people who completely filtered ambiguous situations. They reframed all the evidence of ambiguity into some other, to them plausible, cognitively consistent explanation that negated the uncertainty and transplanted a false stability and certainty. In this case, when the merger actually occurred, both managers quickly started to display signs of shock and within days both were signed off with stress-based illnesses. One never returned to work at that company.

The search was now on for those leaders who, in their eyes, lived in a world of certainty. It was not long before more were found, in a completely different situation, on a leadership course the author was co-facilitating.

At the start of the course, the participants, who were expecting a standard leadership training event, were thrown into a highly unusual situation when the facilitators sat down among the group of participants and did not speak. Within minutes of the session starting, a number of reactions became clearly evident. One participant, Jill, stated that this was a waste of time and that she wanted to go back to work. When asked why by another participant, she reiterated that what was happening was a waste of time and that she could be doing something useful. A short time later, when the participants were discussing what was happening and what to do about it, another participant pointed out that they were dealing with an uncertain situation, to which Jill replied, "I don't have uncertain situations in my life."

There was a long silence. Eventually Don, another participant, broke the silence. "What are you talking about, how can you have no uncertainty in your life?"

"I don't, I know everything that is going to happen," Jill asserted and then added what was to be a big clue to her perception. "My entire day is planned out; I know what I am going to do every day and from minute to minute."

"What!" Don exclaimed. "Nothing ever happens that catches you by surprise?"

"No, nothing." Jill was adamant that there was no uncertainty and she kept this view for a long time.

Eventually I asked Jill what this situation was for her. She restated, "A waste of time."

I then asked, "Do you have similar wastes of time in your life?"

She thought for a second, and replied, "Well yes, sure, quite a lot actually."

When asked to describe some of the situations, she started to illustrate circumstances like one of her key members of staff suddenly leaving "for personal reasons," senior management talk of a reorganization, and the computer network crashing during a busy period. They were all categorized as a waste of time. A waste of time but not recognized as uncertainty.

There then followed a series of questions and answers which give good insights into the minds of people who cannot entertain the idea of any ambiguity in their lives:

Q: What would happen if a situation arose that was uncertain or ambiguous?

A: If such a thing were to happen, then I guess there would be chaos.

Q: What does chaos mean to you?

A: That would be awful, simply awful. I mean in chaos no one would know what to do and people would just be wandering around doing all sorts of things.

Q: When you think of chaos, do you get a picture?

A: Oh yes, it's of people walking in every direction, in front of each other, behind each other, in all different directions. There is no pattern or direction, it's total confusion.

Q: What do these people look like?

A: Er, well, they are all wearing grey suits and are faceless.

Q: Are they responding to each other?

A: No they are ignoring each other, just walking their own walk; they are looking directly in front, ignoring each other.

Q: How do you feel looking at this?

A: Tense, very tense. It's unbearable. I just want to sort it out and get them walking in nice straight lines again. I need to stop the confusion. It's unbearable. Sorry, I can't watch anymore, it's too much.

She then shook her head, looked at me directly, and said, "Phew that was awful", and shook her head again.

Q: So what's the problem with ambiguity?

A: It's scary, way too risky.

Q: Risky?

A: Yes risky, scary, frightening, you know.

Q: Ah, so risky is frightening?

A: Of course, yes.

Q: And uncertainty is frightening?

A: Well yes sort of. It's, it's chaos and chaos is frightening, well not frightening exactly but unbearable. It's the thought of not being able to get out of chaos that is frightening. The thought of not being able to get out of chaos is ... well, it's just too much to bear. I couldn't survive if that were to happen. I mean not get out of chaos, can you imagine? Luckily, the world isn't like that. How could we cope, even manage to live if the world was in chaos all the time?

Q: And chaos comes from uncertainty?

A: Uncertainty is chaos, yes.

It is interesting that Jill perceived that ambiguity and chaos are part of the same thing and further that chaos and, importantly, ambiguity are closely linked with the negative emotions of being scared and fearful and a sense of not being able to cope. She also linked risk with ambiguity and fear, summing it up as being "unbearable."

This suggests that Jill was engaged in a process of removing ambiguity and hence reducing or removing the emotion of fear. Better still, if you can't see any uncertainty, then you don't have to remove or reduce the fear in the first place.

When leaders were examined across the range of organizations, remarkably similar attributes were discovered in about 2 percent of leaders.

Mode one reactions to ambiguity 2: Do something else

A variation on the "there is only certainty" theme was discovered after conversations with a police officer and a New York fireman.

The fireman was involved in the 9/11 terrorist outrage in New York. He was in the second tower trying to get to the fire and evacuate the workers in that tower. He climbed the stairs to about the 21st floor and entered an office, where he found a man sitting at his desk trying to get into his email on his computer. The astonished fireman ordered the man to leave and quickly. He then ran on to check the other offices in the building. After the first tower collapsed, the fireman, on his way out, glanced into the office to find the man still at his desk. He ran in and shouted words to the effect of "get out please." The man said he was having problems with his email, it didn't appear to be working and did the fireman know anything about how computers worked. I'll leave the fireman's reply to your imagination. Even in the face of overwhelming evidence, this individual appeared to be trying to maintain certainty in a highly ambiguous situation.

The police officer related a story of a colleague of his, who, having been shot in the jaw in Northern Ireland, fell to the floor in a pool of blood. He then immediately got back up, opened his pocket book and filled in the date, time, and place of the incident (standard police procedure) before he collapsed from lack of blood. The fireman and policeman survived, by the way.

When sharing these stories with a friend, a zoologist, he told me about a similar phenomenon in the natural world known as "displacement behavior." This usually occurs in the wild when an animal is torn between a fight or flight response. Some birds, like the sparrow, when flying, if they are confronted with the possibility of being caught and eaten by a bird of prey, will sometimes start to preen themselves while in midair. Clearly this interferes with their ability to fly away or put up a defense.

Similar patterns of displacement behavior were discovered in some leaders. For example, one leader, when told there was a strong possibility that his department might be closed imminently unless some urgent and radical change was made to save the situation, went and sat outside the director's office and started to do the crossword in the newspaper in the waiting area. Many similar stories were told and observations made of people staring into the face of uncertainty who went shopping, started to play computer games obsessively, or just continued with their normal life as if nothing was happening. The interviews revealed a similar fear factor to the previous group of leaders described above, the leaders had quickly become overloaded by the uncertainty of the situation. This appears to cause a new rationale to appear in the minds of the individuals concerned, which displaces the negative emotions of the moment and makes it "alright," providing cognitive consistency.

Interestingly, when interviewed about their situation, all the displacement seekers were aware that they were in ambiguous circumstances, saying, for example:

"Yes it's a tough situation and I'm not sure what will happen."

"It's a nightmare scenario; there is no 'win' here. It's a totally lose/lose situation."

"It's really difficult to know what to do. I certainly can't see how to resolve this and I don't think that I'm particularly unintelligent. The company has got itself into a real mess on this one."

"I don't know what to tell my people. Anything might happen next. Until senior management make up their minds, what can I do? I can hardly go in there and tell the troops that I don't know what's going on, can I?"

The clue as to why these people engage in displacement activity was discovered during the initial analysis of the interviews. It was found that all the replies, like the last two above, indicated a feeling of helplessness and a sense that they as leaders were meant to provide certainty to their people and couldn't. One manager, who was found looking through a large pile of holiday brochures while his section sat in another building with no work to do because of changes elsewhere in the organization, stated:

"What can I do? I don't even know what's happening. Am I meant to go over there and tell them that I don't know what to do or what's happening? The job's finished and I'm trapped in the middle. Until someone tells me what's going on and what we are meant to do, what can I do? Look, I've been here almost 17 years; you'd have thought that one of our great leaders would have told us what was happening. I'm as much in the dark as anyone."

Q: "Have you let the senior management know how you feel?"

A: "Hang on a minute; it's not my job to go up there and tell them how to do things, is it? I mean, leadership is about telling people what to do, isn't it? Sod-all leadership around here, I can tell you. So I can hardly go and tell my people what's happening and what to do if I don't know."

All the people engaging in displacement activities similarly reported a unimodal model of leadership, a feeling of helplessness, that others were at fault, and that they were powerless to act.

The research found that the number of leaders engaging in displacement activities was slightly higher, at around 8 percent of the population.

Mode one reactions to ambiguity 3: If in doubt, fool yourself

While the reaction of some mode one leaders to ambiguity is not to recognize the uncertainty of a situation at all, or to engage in displacement activities instead of facing the uncertainty, the next most common response is to deny the uncertainty of the situation that the individual faces. This is usually done by simplifying the ambiguity or deciding that they know what is happening even in the face of contradictory evidence that points to another conclusion.

A good example of this was found during a visit to a police station.

There a senior police officer was briefing some police officers who were about to engage in an operation to arrest a local drugs supplier.

During the briefing, the senior officer gave the address of the house that they were to raid at 5am, later that morning.

"You can't miss it, he lives at number 118, it's a bright red door. He lives on his own and there are no dogs. He is not known to be armed but be careful. Detective Smith has the warrant."

Following the briefing, the officers left the station to take up their positions, surrounding the house in question while the senior officer established herself in the control room to listen in.

At 5am, the senior officer gave the order over the radio to move in. Within seconds, one of the detectives came back and said, "Can you confirm the address please, we're outside number 118 but the door is not red. The red door belongs to number 120, next door."

"Impossible," retorted the boss, "it's 118 and it's the red door. The warrant is for 118, detective."

The detective replied, "Sorry boss, but 118 is a white door and it doesn't look like it's been repainted for a very long time. The bright red door is 120."

"Where is the sergeant? Sergeant, where are you?"

"Sergeant Jones here."

"Go to the front door sergeant and show Detective Smith the right door."

"Yes ma'am."

A few seconds later the sergeant was back on the radio.

"Number 118 is a white door and what's more I can hear a dog barking in there, and the car on the drive has a child's seat in it. Number 120 is the red one, and has no car outside, what do you want us to do?"

"Imbeciles! What street are you in?"

The sergeant responded, "With all due respect ma'am, we are in the correct street. Which door do you want us to go through? If we wait here much longer, they'll be throwing a street party for us."

The senior officer decided, "118 is the number on the warrant, that's the house."

"But," retorted the sergeant, "this looks like a family house. Number 120 is the red door and I can't hear a dog. It looks much more like the thing."

"This is an order; raid 118 like we planned, NOW!"

"Ma'am, I am sure it's the wrong house."

"Just do as you are told, sergeant."

There was a long silence and then the sergeant came back on the radio, with the sound of children crying and a woman shouting in the background. "We have a very frightened woman here with two young children who have just had their front door smashed in and a dozen police officers stampede around their house."

"Search the house, sergeant."

"Sorry? This is the wrong address, these people are just a family."

"I said, search the house, this is the perfect cover for a supplier, and the warrant is for 118, so it must be right."

"I'm stopping this operation now. All officers to R.V. (rendezvous) back at the briefing room immediately. Confirm please," came the reply from the sergeant.

In less dramatic ways, similar responses were observed and heard where leaders simply refused to believe the evidence before them when they found themselves in unfamiliar and uncertain territory. Around 22 percent of leaders in this study were found to respond to ambiguity by plowing on with their original ideas, concepts, and plans, regardless of changes in the situation, new evidence, and even protests from others.

Of these denial leaders, about 95 percent (18 percent of total) of them could not perceive that anything had changed in the situation they faced. When asked to describe the situation a month before and now, these denial leaders all stated that the situation was exactly the same.

The most typical denial response is found at times of individual change like a promotion. Mode one technical leaders are very likely to revert to what they were good at prior to their advancement. In fire officers, this became apparent when quite senior officers were found at the front actually holding the branch (hose) rather than standing back, gathering data and directing others. Mode one police officers become senior constables on promotion, academics become more senior researchers, carrying out their research and teaching as before promotion, the only apparent change being the title and the wages, rather than starting to take some leadership responsibility. Mode one leaders were never found to be taking a strategic view or working towards a vision. They are reactive in behavior, seeing themselves largely as part of the system, waiting to react to orders from above, doing what they did before until told otherwise.

When asked why they had continued in the manner they had, the most frequent rejoinder was:

"Leadership is about leading from the front and making decisions. Regardless of how right or wrong a decision is, someone has to make a decision and that's my job. Their job is to follow and do what they have been told to do and not to question my decisions. If that was allowed, can you imagine the results? Chaos, utter chaos, we'd never get anything done. It's my job to do as I am told and that's what I get paid for, and they get paid to do what I tell them to do and no arguments."

The difference between a denial response and a "certainty" response is that in the denial response the individual or team recognize that they have an emotional response to the uncertainty. This emotional response leads to the person having negative feelings associated with ambiguity and responding by reverting to the more comfortable behaviors or habits associated with there being no ambiguity present. They report feeling, and display the physiology of, discomfort throughout the ambiguous event. Also, when they later reflect on the event, the same feelings become evident.

On the other hand, those who assert that their lives are only constructed of sure, tried and true situations do not even notice the uncertainty. Their emotional response is brief, then it appears that a largely cognitive rationale quickly takes over and the individual typically rationalizes the situation as a "waste of time" and then experiences and notices only the certainty of the situation. These individuals not only fail to recognize the uncertainty inherent in the presenting situation, but they have the feelings of comfort associated with certainty throughout the event.

Problem solving and mode one leadership

In an office, five people sit around a table, cups of coffee steaming next to them. The head of faculty straightened himself in his chair at the head of the table.

"Alright gentlemen, let's get going. We have a lot to cover at this meeting and some decisions to make. As you are all aware, while we generally have a good research team here and some world-class researchers, the quality is not the same across the faculty. We are coming under increasing pressure from other research departments both in the university sector and outside. We need to raise our game and achieve world-class research across the board. To this end, I have decided that from next term each member of staff will keep a diary in which they will record their activities, time spent on research, research proposals, teaching, income generation, and so on – everything they do in fact. This will sharpen their minds as to how they are spending their time and enable us to see what they are doing and sort out those who are just coasting."

The rest of the meeting was taken up by a discussion about how the scheme was going to be implemented and how they, the managers, were going to enforce compliance in a culture not noted for acquiescence. At no time were there any questions about other ideas, nor any attempt to involve or engage the wider community in the issue. Further, there was no consideration aired about the effect the measure would have on the faculty, including those who were already seen as world class, nor was there any exploration of the attributes that contributed to a researcher being seen as "world class" or even ordinary.

An examination of teams' problem-solving strategies showed that those with mode one leaders all tended to defer to the leaders' solutions to problems or use the problem-solving structures laid down by the leader. Further, the problems successfully tackled by mode one leaders and their teams tend to be what Heifetz refers to as "type I" or technical problems.[1] Heifetz proposed three problem types:

1   *Type I or technical problems.* These are problems to which there are standard preworked solutions which just require application, by an expert or experienced individual, of the correct resolution to solve. Problems with decision-making trees are examples of such problems. Technical problems are discussed in detail below.

2   *Type II or cooperative problems.* Simply the solution to this type of problem requires some form of cooperation between people or teams. Cooperative problems are discussed in detail in Chapter 5.

3   *Type III or adaptive problems.* This type of problem requires that the individuals concerned adapt to the circumstances rather than making the problem go away as the other two types attempt to do. Adaptive problems are discussed in detail in Chapter 6.

4   *Type IV or generative problems.* Not part of Heifetz's typology, the generative problem was developed as part of the work for this

book. These are a special category of problem where the problem definition is not really understood or clarified and they tend to be problems that have not yet occurred. Chapter 7 discusses generative problems and solutions in greater detail.

All of these problem types are also examined in some detail in Chapter 8. Type I problems are those that can be solved by an expert by applying standard problem-solving techniques on their own. These tend to be normal workplace problems that are mostly encountered in day-to-day working. They are usually solved by well-founded and standard actions. Examples of such problems include a banker agreeing a loan for a new customer, a police officer dealing with a speeding motorist, a doctor diagnosing and treating an infection, or a mechanic detecting and fixing an engine fault. They are the sorts of technical problems where members of the public typically use the expertise of the practitioner to solve a problem for them. Such problem-solving processes can usually be represented by a flow or decision chart.

The problem arises for mode one teams and leaders when the presenting problem is outside the normal everyday technical challenges.

For example, in 2001 a flying instructor at a Minnesota flight school became concerned when a student enrolled and paid cash to receive instruction on their Boeing 747 simulator. The student Zacarias Moussaoui presented himself to the school after having completed over 50 hours of instruction, but he hadn't yet completed a solo flight on even the smallest light aircraft. The instructor couldn't understand why he now wanted to learn to fly such a large commercial aircraft. He further aroused suspicion by refusing instruction on taking off and landing the aircraft. The instructor reported Moussaoui to the FBI who arrested him in August 2001 for immigration offences. An FBI employee Coleen Rowley, investigating the unusual circumstances, sent a number of requests to FBI headquarters for a warrant to search Moussaoui's property and computer. These requests were refused. The events and deaths of 2,986 people on September 11, 2001 when terrorists hijacked four commercial airliners showed that Rowley was right to be suspicious. Two of the aircraft were piloted into the World Trade Center in New York, one dived into the Pentagon and the third crashed in Shanksville.

Rowley sent a memo to FBI Director Robert S. Mueller in May

2002, alleging that FBI headquarters had deliberately blocked the requests for a warrant:

"Although I agree that it's very doubtful that the full scope of the tragedy could have been prevented, it's at least possible we could have gotten lucky and uncovered one or two more of the terrorists in flight training prior to September 11."

She also asserted that "certain facts have been omitted, downplayed, glossed over and/or mischaracterized" in the report about why the threat had not been identified before the attacks.

These responses to the agent's requests are typical mode one thinking system reactions to ambiguity and solving ambiguous problems, especially the ambiguity presented when a mode one leader's model of the world is in conflict with the presenting evidence. The dissonance caused usually results in some form of denial, whereby the individual changes the meaning of the evidence to return the world back to the world which works nicely with their thinking paradigm. They have a strong drive for cognitive consistency.

Mode one approaches to diversity

"Well, I think that the first candidate certainly has all the qualifications."

"Yes and so does the third guy really."

"I know but will he fit in here?"

"I know what you mean. Comes over as very efficient and has great references, but he's a bit, you know, a bit humorless."

"Yes, quite serious really. I'm not sure that he will enjoy working with us. We tend to like a bit of a laugh really."

"The first woman, what's her name? She was much better; she came over as quite human."

"Yes, a much better fit. I also thought that her way of thinking was much more like ours. I do think that she would get on well here. Quite like us really."

"OK, that's agreed then."

"Yes I think so, even though, er, Jim is it? Yes Jim, even though he is very well qualified and could certainly do the job, I agree that he wouldn't be very happy here and I don't think that he would fit in."

"No, she is much more like us and getting someone who will be part of the team is very important."

Mode one teams and leaders tend toward the safety of similarity, especially during recruiting where characteristics that appear to make a candidate "one of us" are most likely to be the deciding factor in their favor.

Additionally, where an existing member of a team does not conform to the norms of the group or tries to highlight a problem that creates an ambiguous situation, it is almost certain that efforts will be made to compel the errant individual to fall back in line, conform, and not "create" problems or uncertainty.

One of the most famous examples of mode one marginalization of a nonconformist team member's views (and their reaction to the uncertainty created by that individual) happened in a series of events over a year from January 1985 to January 1986 which led up to the NASA *Challenger* disaster on January 28, 1986. The year before the accident, Roger Boisjoly, one of the engineers, questioned whether the O-rings, which joined the sections of the rocket boosters that the shuttle was attached to, were safe at the temperatures being experienced on the launch pad. Finally, exasperated by not being listened to by his management, he committed his expert opinion to a written memo to his leaders that ended, "It is my honest and very real fear that if we do not take immediate action to dedicate a team to solve the problem, with the field joint having number one priority, then we stand in jeopardy of losing a flight along with all the launch pad facilities."[2]

The response from Boisjoly's bosses at NASA was to give him strict instructions to stop his claims of the critical urgency of the situation and he was later ordered not to refer to it in future communications or presentations. A series of incidents then occurred in which management reduced Boisjoly's influence and authority, until the actual disaster. These days Boisjoly concentrates on helping other engineers to make and stand by ethical decisions.[3]

The picture here is of leaders with a very low tolerance for ambiguity and a high need for structure. Any changes they make tend to be small, incremental, and adaptions of current practice or products.

They are very good in situations with little variation that require the application and reapplication of learnt and standardized responses where problem solving is mainly formulaic.

5 Mode Two: Cooperative Leadership

Great discoveries and improvements invariably involve the cooperation of many minds. I may be given credit for having blazed the trail but when I look at the subsequent developments I feel the credit is due to others rather than to myself. Alexander Graham Bell, Scottish inventor (1847–1922)

Mode two leadership scenarios are identifiable by a call for cooperation between the team members. The preoccupation of these leaders and teams is a drive toward teamwork and getting people to work together. Unlike mode one leaders, mode two leaders are interested in and actively seek the opinions of the team. They also promote cooperation with other teams and frequently endorse that they work in cooperation with their customers.

The motivation for cooperative forms of work appears to be the recognition that in comparison to mode one leadership, the idea of collecting the views of the team increases the chances of the "right" answer coming up and spreads or minimizes any risk of failure. While on the face of it mode two leaders would go with the consensus of the group, in reality they "facilitate" the best answer to their scheme. The strategy of the mode two leader is to minimize risk, based on the principle that many heads are better than one and that the leader uses the resources of the team to further their work agenda. They realize that they need the cooperation of subordinates in the workplace in order to achieve their outcomes. While, like the mode one leader, they still have a wish for conformity from their staff, they tend to use more subtle ways of gaining this. Tending to be less likely to resort to direct confrontation or orders, cooperative leaders are more likely to appeal to an individual's sense of group conformity and the wish not to stand out from team norms. While they will only rarely use brute power or rank to affect compliance, they will however resort to such behavior when things are not going their way, or group cohesion is fractured. In contrast, the technical leader would use power most of the time, whereas cooperative leaders will usually only do so when more influential methods have failed. Compliance of the team members, like the mode one leader, is still a prime concern, however the method of achieving acquiescence usually comes from a realization that a volunteer is better than someone who has been overtly obliged to comply. This is attained by sponsoring cooperative working to make the best of the mind resources available and encourage everyone to engage in problem solving. The main orientation of mode two teams, like that of their technical counterparts, is an "away from" focus on reducing the risk of failure and thus, it is believed, increasing the certainty of success.

A considerable amount of effort is directed into team building. Performance problems are usually ascribed to a lack of team cohesion or individuals who don't fit within the team ideal. Perversely, and almost as a result of this focus, mode two teams are more likely to be in conflict than any other type of grouping. This is largely because most calls for cooperation are made for functional reasons rather than for genuine exploration of individuals' differences and differing value sets. That said, the potency of the structures they construct is to spread and minimize risk through strength in numbers, often enabling the team to choose the best solutions available to this paradigm.

Mode two problem solving

The weakness in this system is that such teams and the leader usually go after the safe bet, the solution that is most likely to give an acceptably profitable result with the least risk possible. Consequently, innovative and highly advantageous ideas are rarely pursued. Such teams and their leaders are usually good at solving both technical type I and type II problems, where cooperation with the client is needed to resolve an issue or where working with other teams is needed for the successful conclusion of an issue. Problem solving will usually be research-led and based on a careful, systematic analysis of the evidence in search of "the" answer. It is highly unlikely that multiple answers will be permitted to emerge – in a drive for certainty, considerable effort will be made to find the one, correct solution. The tried and tested solution is usually the result that will be chosen over and above any option that is a new and innovative solution, especially if there is no certainty that it will work, which, by their very nature, is almost always the case for new solutions.

The contestant's dilemma

Consider the following example that happened recently on a quiz show in the U.K.

A man had won 100,000 random lottery tickets during the show. Each ticket has a 1 in 54 chance of winning some form of prize. The odds for each prize are as follows:

£2,000,000   – 1 in 14,000,000
£100,000   – 1 in 2,400,000
£1,500   – 1 in 55,500
£50   – 1 in 1,000
£10   – 1 in 57

The lucky winner also won £40,000 in cash. At the end of the show he had to make a choice. He could either elect to keep the £40,000 cash he had won and give the lottery tickets to another contestant, who would then get whatever the tickets had won, or he could keep the lottery tickets and see there and then what they had won and take that money home and give the guaranteed £40,000 to the other contestant.

- A risk-averse person would take the £40,000.
- A risk-neutral person would say it didn't matter and choose one at random.
- A risk taker would take the tickets to discover how much they had won.

He decided to keep the £40,000 and give the tickets to the other contestant, who then went on to win over £250,000!

The contestant displayed all the characteristics of a mode two leader and team member, taking the safe course of action even though there was a good possibility of a higher reward, especially given the fact that he had actually walked in with nothing. While in most cases this will give a modest return, it is unlikely to lead to solutions to problems that are adaptive or predictive in nature, both of which require risk-taking behavior.

Mode two reactions to diversity

Mode two teams and particularly mode two leaders, due to their concern for compliance and reduction of conflict, emphasize similarity and equality in team members. The espoused philosophy of "we are all equals and individuals" recognizes individual differences but also stresses a level of egalitarianism. This position creates a contradiction for the mode two leader. On the one hand, they want similarity in team members, like the mode one leader, but they also recognize that this is impossible to achieve and that the individuals in their teams or organization are different. Difference is seen as a cause of conflict, the logic usually being that different people, different values, and diverse values can cause interpersonal conflict. Therefore, in an attempt to reduce any potential for conflict, mode two leaders resort to promoting equality and reducing differences where possible without offending members of the team. So diversity is tolerated where necessary but is really undesirable, and that diversity can be on any level – thinking, background, ethnicity, schooling, qualifications, and dress. Almost anything that signifies difference can be seen as a potential threat to the stability of the team.

The mode two leader and ambiguity

As will be extrapolated from the profile thus far of a modal mode two cooperative leader, ambiguity, like risk and diversity, is not welcomed. While it is accepted as a fact of life, it is seen as something to be controlled and minimized to ensure continuance of their prime concern – stability. It is this quality that mode two leaders believe is the linchpin to success. When things are stable, they can predict what actions will consistently lead to what outcomes. This predictability allows them to know the rules – the rules of how to operate and make a profit, the rules of cause and effect. Follow the rules and make a profit. Mode two leaders are those most likely to read biographies of successful leaders to ascertain the rules of leadership and success.

In situations of ambiguity of any type, the mode two leader will tend to try to simplify the situation and reduce it to a series of rules and is likely to create a system or policy, often bureaucratic, to prevent and reduce any uncertainty.

Colin leads a team of engineers who have been working on fuel
tank design for a new type of aircraft. During the research phase, a
number of different materials needed to be tested for their ability
to self-seal in the event of a puncture. The team was instructed to
locate a variety of these new materials from a number of
manufacturers for testing to evaluate their suitability for use. When
the materials start to arrive, it becomes apparent that two orders
have been made in error, which, by the time the correct materials
arrive, will have caused a significant delay to the project. As a result,
Colin designed a system whereby *all* orders are double-checked
and then need to be authorized by a supervisor. The new system
was formalized as a new policy to be applied in every case. The
group had been working without many errors for more than 12
years up to this point. It is estimated that this new policy now
consumes approximately 350–400 hours a year in extra
administration and double-checking, which is equivalent to 50 days
of one person's production per year for what is estimated to be
about 12–15 ordering errors a year, resulting in delays estimated to
be no more than two weeks' worth of production over a year.
When examined, many of the errors are on nonsystem critical
items like stationery.

The unsolvable mode two leadership problem

Commercial entities, noncommercial organizations, such as universities, and service industries, like the police, health services and so on,
all at some time face the familiar problem of not having enough
profit or income to meet the needs of the service or company to carry
on doing what it is currently doing. The usual mode two systematic
response to reduce costs and overheads, restructure, and start or
increase outsourcing will work for a while. This sort of scenario is seen
by mode two players as a typical type II cooperative problem – get
people to cooperate to reduce costs, leave and/or work differently.
However, a reality for mode two leaders is that such cooperative
solutions, while they can be effective a couple of times, soon reach
the point where cost-cutting exercises become counterproductive.
Cutting training and development budgets, for instance, is usually
done exactly when employees need support to change how they are

working, and a good training program could help to deliver the required change more quickly than leaving the workers to "get on with it."

Leaders who are stuck in mode two will keep seeing type II problems, applying the same cooperative solutions until either they lose their jobs, their company or external events move things on, or a happy accident happens to revive their fortunes until the next time. In order to cope with the conflict created by cooperative practices, mode two leaders may start to seek other ways to work that will reduce the conflict. They may, for example, regress to mode one and try to tighten controls and become ever more dictatorial, usually causing a sudden surge in staff turnover and the resultant costs, which could finish the company or organization. Alternatively, they might transition into mode three. Of course many will remain in mode two, become stuck and learn to live with or ignore the conflicts inherent in mode two working.

For each of the modes, there will be those in transition in one direction or the other, or those who are stuck in any mode or transitional position either permanently or temporarily.

Mode Three: Adaptive/ Collaborative Leadership

*I have always thought that the best way to find out what is right
and what is not right, what should be done and what should not
be done, is not to give a sermon, but to talk and discuss, and
out of discussion sometimes a little bit of truth comes out.*
Jawaharlal Nehru, Indian statesman (1889–1964)

Mode three leaders are discernible by their concern with collaboration as opposed to the cooperative focus of mode two. The differences are that while mode two leaders focus on reducing conflict
primarily by placing an emphasis on individuals burying their differences, mode three leaders recognize the differences between people
and realize that conflict is an inherent and important part of life. The
outcome of this is that mode three leaders spend considerable time
dealing with and exploring conflict to enable individuals to work
through the conflict and gain an understanding of themselves, how
others see and react to them and further learn to appreciate the value
of others through that conflict. Mode three is where diversity starts
to become understood as a real strength and is accepted as part and
parcel of work life. In short, these leaders are more able to adapt to
local conditions and respond positively to change and conflict,
moving into a new place rather than reacting by merely trying to
control things.

Mode three risk behavior

Another defining moment for an emerging mode three leader is the
realization that with risk comes the possibility of enhanced rewards
and the emphasis moves from the risk reduction of mode two
thinking to an exploration of the risks involved. As the individual
moves more toward modal mode three, they actually start looking to

take risks that will give them the upper hand. At first, the new mode three leader, in transition between modes two and three, will be motivated to try to find "sensible" risks to take – risks where the odds are stacked firmly in their favor. They will conduct a lot of research to give them confidence that the risk is a reasonably safe bet. As they gain experience and confidence, particularly if they see others taking bigger risks and reaping bigger rewards, they will start to enhance their risk taking. Some leaders, it has to be said, also appear to be comfortable with risk taking straight away and start taking bets on things that can often frighten those who have come with them from previous, safer shores. Many, however, need to wean themselves off risk reduction slowly and have a series of positive experiences of risk-taking behavior. This does not mean that the bets they make all have to work, but that the environment they work in needs to be mistake- and failure-tolerant. The understanding in teams with modal mode three leaders is that mistakes and failures are all part of the process and they are as valuable learning events as successes, and often more so. As a leader moves toward the boundary with mode four, there is a growing implicit understanding that innovation, problem solving, and risk go hand in hand. As they move from the safe, overly researched bets toward more truly innovative and open solutions, they start to create an environment where their staff can feel safe and free to collaborate on idea generation.

Mode three problem solving

Mode three adaptive/collaborative leaders' concerns tend to turn increasingly toward the creation of an environment where innovation and risk are encouraged to solve current problems. They adapt to the current situation and most importantly construct innovative solutions.

An example of a low (mode two to three transition) mode three leadership intervention was seen in 1989 at the car manufacturer Mazda.

Mazda realized that it needed something new to get it out of a worsening sales situation in the face of some strong competition in its traditional market segments. It set two teams of designers against each other in a winner-takes-all competition. One team in Japan and one in the United States were given the task of coming up with a car design that would move the company forward. This resulted in a number of designs, one of which produced one of the most popular and highest selling sports cars in the world, the Mazda MX5 (Miata).

There was a realization by the leadership of Mazda that an approach beyond that of the traditional cuts, reductions, restructuring, and outsourcing was required to adapt to the new world of the global car market and world conditions at the time. It needed to find an adaptive solution to the new world conditions in which it found itself. Adaptive solutions require change; a change in thinking, values, and in actions. Although at first sight the Mazda solution appears to be anything but collaborative, a closer consideration of what had to happen within the leadership, between the leadership and each of the teams, and within each of the teams to adapt to the new situation and find a solution, highlights the collaboration involved.

The problem types that adaptive/collaborative leaders excel in are adaptive problems, whereby a solution either cannot be found or is unpalatable for some reason. These are known as "type III problems" and they require some form of adaptation in order to be resolved. For example, a patient who has an incurable condition or a car owner who is told that his or her car is beyond repair by the mechanic – both the patient and the driver have to adapt to the situation.

Collaboration vs cooperation

In normal usage, cooperation and collaboration are often used interchangeably and without distinction. In this book, however, a distinction has been drawn between the two. Collaboration is everything that is required for the act of working together for a common and, most importantly, an agreed purpose. This includes sharing responsibility for the processes and outcomes of the endeavor. On the other hand, cooperation intimates that while there are differing agendas and values, the actors involved agree to suspend their differences to enable the completion of the task. There is a palpable tension that exists in a cooperative environment due to the suppressed differing agendas that live in cooperative societies. Collaborative settings, however, are denoted by similar agendas and values. This is no happy accident but is designed, based on the understanding that mode three leaders have about dealing with interpersonal issues or processes. This practice helps to align individuals' values and their resultant agendas, which reduces tensions within teams.

Mode three and ambiguity

Ambiguous situations are tolerated much better by mode three leaders than mode one and two leaders and their teams because of the adaptive and change-oriented nature of their outlook. They recognize that controlling and changing the conditions within which they exist is usually and eventually futile. New worlds cannot be ignored, reduced, or denied, the only option is to adapt to the conditions and change what is being done. A typical maxim of mode three leaders is "if you always do what you've always done, you'll always get what you always got." If you need a different outcome to the one you have, then do something different – more of the same (modes one and two) will not achieve it.

When mode three leaders face an ambiguous situation, first, they see the data with little distortion, deletion, or generalization. They have a high degree of self-understanding and will often notice and diminish their own filtering. This means that their analysis is likely to show that there has been a change in their life conditions, in short that a new world has dawned, which requires new thinking and new behaviors. Second, they are adaptable. They usually cope with the dissonance caused by change and put their efforts into finding solutions that are not based on old solutions – new worlds need new answers. They are less likely than mode one and two leaders to be victims of the phenomenon of cognitive consistency.

Mode three teams and their leaders are creative, usually generating many good new ideas and they have the ability to operate in circumstances of ambiguity for extended periods. However, while their output of ideas is high, the transmission of ideas into artifacts can be low. The mode three individual is essentially an ideator.[1] As a leader, their drive is directed toward solving problems and the ecology of current situations. This means that the mode three leader is trying to discover the natural balance for their team and their organization and the systems in which they exist.

This idea of a natural balance appears to be at the heart of their acceptance of the situation or context, which allows mode three thinkers to explore the world and find out what it is really like before making a judgment or reacting emotionally and trying to impose their structure about the way the world works. They are less likely to enforce their models on the world by deleting, distorting, or generalizing the information as mode one and many mode two individuals would. While it is impossible to be free of this process entirely, mode three players are much more likely to be aware of the order that they are placing on the world and to compensate for this. In effect, this means that they are more likely than their mode one or two counterparts to recognize a situation and the ambiguities contained within it, and furthermore to be more accepting of and comfortable with the fact that there are uncertainties inherent in almost any situation. The unknown intrigues the modal mode three leader, who is keen to unravel and understand the ambiguity in order to discover how to restore equilibrium, which they see helps with creating the correct environment within which to arrive at a consensus.

Mode three consensus

To solve the conflict problems faced by cooperative leadership styles, the ideal of consensual leadership is personal, professional, and team growth. As the consensual processes mature, the conflict that was apparent under the mode two regime starts to melt away. This reward enhances the new mode three leader's commitment to consensus, and more and more work becomes teamwork as the mode three leader focuses on collaboration, harmony, and acceptance. Diversity and inclusive practices form the bedrock of mode three leaders as they emphasize the need for shared vision and values, and a real sense of "team."

As this happens, a number of other side effects become apparent. Employees, clients, and other customer groups feel really valued and welcomed by the modal mode three team. As a result, mode three leaders have a real feel for the needs of customers or clients and can "read" them very well. The problem arises when others, particularly other teams, don't share the mode three ideal of the collective. A self-seeking or ambitious individual in a mode three team will quickly find themselves ostracized, and other groups or clients who just want to get down to business (mode two) or the mode one authoritarian approach will soon find that the touchy-feely mode three leader or team have become less than inviting. So while consensus seeking is a prime activity of the mode three leader, anyone who constantly blocks or frustrates the process may find themselves marginalized or, at worst, eventually removed from the process altogether.

Mode three leadership and development

A typical mode three leader usually believes that there is potential in anyone to do anything. An example of this type of thinking is apparent in the book *Animals, Inc.* where the animals take over the running of a farm.[2] This belief that everyone has the same potential to achieve anything results in some hilarious outcomes in the book, whereby the mice get to drive the tractor (if only they could), the cat who wants to be a manager ends up managing the mice, with predictable results, and the scarecrow leaves his job of guarding his field full of seeds in the hands of a crow to go and fulfill his dreams and do something more advanced – laying eggs in the hen house, again with foreseeable results.

The mode three leader will often be found spreading valuable resources evenly across a team when better effects could be achieved by concentrating development and training on those strategically placed to benefit the organization or situation. Herein lies the great weakness of mode three leaders, a lack of discernment with their staff and others, leading to excessive costs for minimal or no gain. This often happens to the detriment of the organization and the individuals involved, where more hardnosed and pragmatic judgments can build on strengths rather than spending time trying to minimize weaknesses or obtain equality. For mode three individuals, diversity is really about equality, in the belief that we need to accept everyone's differences because underneath we are all the same, part of the human race.

The problem mode three leaders face that they can't solve adequately is that the consensual processes, the sense of inclusiveness, and the good feelings of their customers have all been created, at a high cost, in terms of time, resources, and often money. Mode three leaders and their teams quickly run out of time and the costs tend to be high. Additionally, as time and costs are the Achilles heel of the mode three leader, eventually customers can lose patience, especially if delays are substantial. Another dual problem the mode three leader faces is that getting consensual agreement frequently means that some of the team have to give up their own ideals to achieve the consensus. In short, what on the surface often appears to be a consensus is in fact a tradeoff of principles and standards. This then leads to the second dilemma; the closer the members of a team get to each other, the more there is a need by the members to be individuals and stand out. As this goes against the ideal of consensual teams, pressure, usually in the form of peer pressure, is exerted on the team members who are starting to express their individuality, particularly if that individualism threatens the ideals of equality, consensual working practices, and sense of group cohesion. If the erring team member persists, they are likely to find themselves marginalized and, in extreme cases, removed from their position of influence or indeed their job.

Eventually, the number of team members who start to show individualistic tendencies often increases, to the extent that the very ideals of the mode three group and leader are in jeopardy of breaking down completely.

The problem adaptive/collaborative leaders face that they can't solve is how to deal with the rise of individualism, which threatens consensual and collaborative working. Additionally, when solving problems they are usually still bound by more traditional problem-solving strategies.

Mode Four: Generative Leadership

The search for static security – in the law and elsewhere – is misguided. The fact is ... security can only be achieved through constant change, through discarding old ideas that have outlived their usefulness and adapting to current facts. **William Orville Douglas, U.S. Supreme Court** associate justice, 1935–75, professor of law at Yale

The move from mode three to mode four leadership is, unlike the previous transitions, not linear, instead the transition to mode four is a seismic shift in thinking, beliefs, and behaviors, a true paradigm shift. Mode four leaders see, analyze, and solve problems in ways that frequently cause others problems, as they often "break the rules" of the other three modes and yet can move easily to any of these, using their thinking approaches when necessary, and, if required, they can create new solutions fashioned from elements of each of the other modes. Additionally, mode four leaders are the most flexible and innovative of all leaders. They are like learning machines with the ability to create and evaluate new ideas, integrating them into current schemes of thinking, and can let go of knowledge that does not suit the current conditions. This ability to readily forgo previous learning that is not working in a current context or world sets the generative leader apart from all other leaders, who will hold onto obsolete learning in spite of clear evidence that even the knowledge of the past must die along with the old world that created it. In transition from mode three to four, leaders often start the transition out of three by trying any new leadership fad that offers solutions to their problems. Those who have the largest and most objective[1] capacity to learn will make the transition, those with a limited or more subjective capacity to learn and unlearn rapidly are unlikely to move into mode four. Modal mode four individuals are the masters of complexity (see Chapter 3) and are inveterate experimenters and educated risk takers.

Although relatively rare – approximately 1.6 percent of leaders discovered have been in this arena – their impact is usually massive. It should be noted at this point that mode four individuals, like those in other modes, may not necessarily be in formal leadership roles. However, if a mode four individual is not in a formal leadership position, they will still be leading by influence. These individuals are described as quietly loud, they ask the questions or add a perspective that changes people's thinking. Rarely interested in the limelight and frequently embarrassed by the attention they can get, these individuals are highly creative and pragmatic.

As true innovators they will think nothing of breaking any rules that appear to them to be getting in the way of the solution, and usually frustrate the hell out of individuals and functions within organizations like HR who are trying to create order and do things right. Mode four leaders will often ignore policies and do the right thing for the situation and the people, creating their own rules. They will tend to create teams of individuals based on their strengths or expertise and will ignore, sideline, and eventually remove nonperformers; they do not suffer fools, or people who do not contribute positively, gladly. On the other hand, they will reward people who perform well in a number of ways and will invest heavily in their development.

The mode four team (usually a mode four leader and mode one, two and three individuals) will look chaotic from the outside, with individuals apparently doing their own thing and acting more like an army of private consultants than a homogeneous team. Indeed, the mode four leader will treat them all like professional consultants, regardless of their position, and the emphasis is on autonomy and independence. This can cause problems for individuals new to the team who expect a lot of direction and supervision. There will hardly ever be any supervision, instead individuals are expected to be proactive and get on with their jobs professionally. Mistakes are not tolerated in mode four teams; they are *expected* and even welcomed as part of the experimental culture they try to create. As long as team members actively analyze and learn from any mistakes, it is unlikely that the leader will even mention it as a mistake.[2] Indeed, the focus is on learning, and individuals who are self-deceptive, overly defensive or blame others, for example, are usually given the opportunity to change. If they don't, they are likely to be removed quickly and the team will move on without them. The anathema to a mode four leader is stability and a lack of progression and learning. These people are hounds of change who learn and expect others to learn and progress constantly. They create change continually and quickly, always moving forward and out; exploring boundaries and possibilities. Life in a mode four team is exciting, innovative, very busy, and complex.

Mode four leaders are usually *polychronic*, with many different projects on the go at one time, and appear from the outside to apportion time and resources between the ventures haphazardly.[3] This is not the case. They are apportioning time based on "this is the best time to move on this." Also, and as a result of this approach, they make linkages between jobs and see relationships and connections others would miss. It also means that they are immensely flexible and will drop a project if it appears not to be going to achieve what they want. As a result they can appear to respond incredibly quickly to situations as events change but very slowly on some projects when viewed from a traditional, linear project management or project completion "tick box" perspective. This can be frustrating for the more structured thinkers within an organization, particularly if the others are in fact trying to manage a mode four individual.

These are the individuals in an organization who appear to do quite well gaining responsibility early but people don't quite know why. They don't play by the rules, take shortcuts, are insightful, and influential in a quiet way.

Mode four problem solving

The first thing to note about mode four problem solving is that it does not fit within Heifetz's types of problem (see Chapter 4). Heifetz stops at adaptive problems, those problems which require an adaptation of the people involved to mitigate the problem. Mode four goes several steps further than adaptation. While mode four leaders can deal with any of the three types of problems Heifetz talks about – technical, cooperative and adaptive – they work on problems in an entirely different way to the previous three modes.

How generative individuals perceive problems and solutions

To gain an insight into how generative individuals perceive the task of problem solving, we need to look at problems in terms of the nature of the energy used to solve them, separate out the problems from their symptoms, and understand their relationship to time (Figure 7.1).

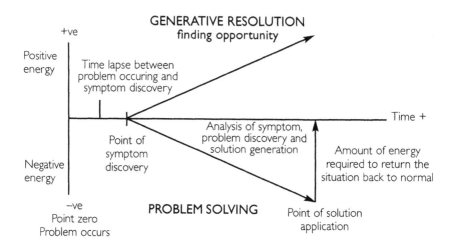

Figure 7.1 Problem solving and generative resolution

The vertical line marked point zero is the point in time at which a problem occurs and runs from positive energy at the top through neutral energy in the middle to negative energy at the bottom.

Negative energy is defined as the energy used to solve a problem, the solution to which merely returns us to the state we were in before the problem occurred. Positive energy is that which is used to take the issue to a completely different place where new opportunities emerge, and does not merely return the situation to where it was before the problem occurred. Neutral energy is the point at which no action is being taken in relation to the problem and thus no energy is being expended.

The horizontal axis marked time dissects the vertical line at the neutral energy point and represents the time elapsed since the moment the problem occurs.

When a problem occurs, it is rare for it to be noticed immediately in any complex system. Usually people perceive the symptoms first and these will always occur *after* the problem has occurred. Then there will be a period of time while the symptoms are analyzed and the under-pinning problem tracked down. So, for example, when a car breaks down, it is usual to discover that the breakdown is actually a symptom of some problem that started some time ago but wasn't noticed until the performance of the engine changed. The longer the length of time between the problem occurring, the symptoms being noticed and the problem being correctly diagnosed, the more likely it is that the problem has become more acute, and as such will normally require more energy to resolve the situation and bring it back to normal.

Mode one, two and three individuals generally engage in this type of problem solving whereby the aim of solving problems is to return the situation back to the preproblem state. Generative leaders, on the other hand, frequently employ a different strategy. When the symp-toms are noticed, mode four leaders are quite likely to explore the situation and the environment and then rather than using negative energy to merely bring the situation back to the pre-problem state, they will use positive energy to investigate those opportunities the situation presents and move into a new space.

Generative individuals will rarely accept the problem as presented and will spend a lot of time and mental energy thinking about and exploring the problem definition, or what the problem is. Einstein once famously commented that he spent approximately 80 percent of his time working out what the problem was and 20 percent solving it. These leaders often apparently do nothing to solve the problem from a traditional thinker's perspective. An example of this comes from the 1920s in New York.

The enabling technology that was really at the core of the development of tall buildings and skyscrapers was the advance in lift or elevator equipment. People were able for the first time to travel dozens of levels with little effort. By about 1930, the year in which the foundations for the Empire State Building were started, there were problems with the technology that started to restrict the thinking about the sensible height to which buildings should be erected. The problem was that people were starting to complain that the elevators were too slow. As the buildings got higher, the time people were spending in lifts increased proportionately. The four elevator construction companies in the state were summoned to the mayor's office and asked to solve the problem. The prize for the winner was some quite glittering contracts not only for new building projects but also to replace older, slower systems.

The first company got to work and developed a bigger winding motor that could winch the lifts at a faster rate. The problems they encountered were twofold. First, the weight of the motor made it difficult to get to the top of buildings, resulting in the prohibitively expensive option of building each motor on site. Second, there is a finite speed at which you can accelerate human bodies before they either feel uncomfortable, sick, or bits like ankles start to break. This added to the problems, requiring a gearing system that added to the weight and maintenance costs. They priced themselves out of the market and quickly went out of business.

The second company invested their solution on a dual technological solution comprising a new motor and pulley system. Beset with technical problems due to the complexity of the solution, they ran out of money before they could solve the issue of rates of acceleration of the elevator cars.

The third company, known for its innovation, did just that, innovated. A number of project teams got to work on their parts of the problem. One team looked at the motor power, one at the motor design, one at gearing, one at car design, and so on. The project at that time carried the record for the number of patents from one company. Unfortunately, none of the inventions were quite able to work together and eventually they ran out of time and money as well and were never able to deliver a coherent and reliable product in the timescale required.

The fourth company's chief engineer, who had been summoned by the board and told to solve the problem, went back to his team and explained the task.

On the wall in his office he wrote in large letters

THE ELEVATORS ARE TOO SLOW

He pondered this for a few days, frequently looking at the problem statement. After days of thought, he added to the statement to generate the problem statement:

THEY SAY THAT THE ELEVATORS ARE TOO SLOW

His engineers were asked to go and actually ride in all the elevators they could find and report back.

A week later they all returned and at a meeting he asked what they had found. Three of the engineers found that there was a slight difference in speed between floors of the different makes of elevator but that the difference in speed was minimal. A fourth engineer added that he had asked his family to ride in six elevators and although his stopwatch had shown a difference in speeds, his family members had not been able work out which was actually the fastest.

The chief engineer said that he had noticed an odd thing. Groups of people would often be talking outside the elevator and then when they entered it they would often stop talking or their conversation would become broken with longer pauses.

Puzzled, they headed back to the elevators around the state to find out what people thought of their speed. A week later they reported back. At this stage, the board asked the chief engineer to return with his plans for faster elevators. He said that he was working on the problem but did not have any plans as yet, which did not ease the nerves of the senior managers as they knew that their competitors were now hard at work developing things like bigger motors and gears. However, the chief engineer had been with the company for years and they allowed him to continue.

A week later the engineers met and reported back some very strange things. The first was that they had found it hard to ask people questions while they were riding in the elevator and that people tended not to give very detailed answers. As a result most of the engineers had taken to standing at the top or bottom of the buildings and asking people about the speed of their journey. Most replied that it was too slow and, as many of the office workers had to move between floors during their daily work, this was a real problem.

The second strange thing was that one engineer had persisted with his questions in the elevator. He reported that the people he talked to would look ill at ease and hardly ever made eye contact. However, on the odd occasion he had asked people a whole load of questions during their journey and then got off with them. When they were out of the elevator, he then asked them about the speed of the ride. On these occasions, they said that the ascent or descent was fine unlike those who he had only spoken to outside the elevators.

Another noted that when a stranger got into an elevator people would look at their shoes or the roof of the car. They would only look directly at people they knew. The journeys with people who didn't know each other were mostly completed in silence.

The chief engineer went back to his sentence on the wall and scored out the word say and wrote in the word think.

THEY ~~SAY~~ THINK THAT THE ELEVATORS ARE TOO SLOW

Summoned back to the board, the chief engineer again repeated that his team were still working on the problem and no, he didn't have a plan yet. The board then held a discussion about replacing the chief engineer as this was a critical project that could safeguard the future of the company and they needed a man of action not someone who was conducting social research. The motion was narrowly defeated, mainly on the casting vote of the chairman who said, "I know Tom does some strange things at times and that he doesn't always do what we want him to do, but in over 25 years of knowing him I can say that what he has designed or worked on has never failed. Some of his solutions have appeared pretty odd at the time but 9 times out of 10 they work better than we could have hoped for. I want him to continue for a little while longer. We mustn't be provoked into panic measures just because the other firms appear to be moving forward and we don't."

The chief engineer then did something that even made his own engineers wonder. He sent them all home. "Go for a walk, a drive, see the family, do anything but this. When a solution pops into your head, regardless of what it is, come back and tell us all. I'll see you all on Friday – just don't come back until something comes up. And remember the problem we are trying to solve – he pointed at the wall. The problem appears to be that they *think* that the lifts are too slow. Is this the problem we have to solve?"

When the board heard that the chief engineer had sent his team home for the rest of the week, he was summoned again.

"Look Tom, this is pretty weird even for you. People are starting to lose confidence in you; some are even suggesting that you have finally gone mad."

"Do you trust me Mr. Jameson?", the chief engineer asked.

"Yes I do but this sort of thing is pretty hard to defend to the rest of the board with so much at stake. I don't have to tell you what's at stake here. We can't afford to get this one wrong."

Friday arrived and the engineering office was full of excited chatter as all the engineers arrived back. They took it in turns to say what they thought the problem really was. After much discussion, they concluded that there were a couple of problems. First, people didn't know when they were going to arrive at their floor and that because they were in a confined space, this altered their normal behavior, different, say, from a train or coach trip where they would read or stare out of the window. They realized that the elevator passengers were bored and that a confined space changed their behavior.

"Do we make bigger elevators?" asked one engineer.

"Or," said the chief engineer, "Do we make it look as if the elevator car is bigger?"

The engineers thought about this. The chief engineer asked, "In your house, how do you create the illusion of space in a small room?"

"Well by not painting it dark colors for a start," replied one.

"Good," said the chief engineer, "and what else?"

Someone then shouted, "Of course, mirrors, you put mirrors in a small room!"

"OK, so let's try it. While we are doing this, let's also see what we can do about the actual speed of the elevators."

They quickly tested the idea of light colors and mirrors in an elevator and found that everyone who rode in the elevator thought that the speed had improved but were usually at a loss to say why. The innovation cost a few dollars. Along with modest improvements in speed and a floor indication system, so that everyone in the car could see (above the door) where the elevator was before the doors opened, the elevators appeared to move incredibly quickly. This was all achieved at minimal cost but brought in huge contracts.

This is an excellent example of mode four problem solving in that the chief engineer spent time redefining and reframing the problem definition, to ensure that they were solving the right problem. Also, and importantly, the chief engineer was quite happy to remain in a position of ambiguity and resist the temptation to foreclose on a solution even under pressure from above, while the emergent properties of the situation were found. Open to all possibilities and not happy to accept the "obvious" solutions, compound leaders use the situation to explore and, above all, learn.

Mode four leaders and individuals do not just adapt to current situations like mode three leaders, they innovate their way out of the situation and into a more positive space. Adaptation is a reactive process, once there is a change, mode three collaborative leaders will quickly recognize the change and find a range of solutions, some of which will involve adapting to the new situation. Mode four generative leaders, on the other hand, frequently create change and predict problems.

A further distinction of generative leaders is that they are tolerant of confusion, usually they do not have a problem if all the pieces do not fit together, they are very happy to wait for patterns to emerge; indeed, being polychronic, time is rarely the issue that monochronic individuals face. They will act quickly when things are clear, but understand when they are in a fog and will allow time for emergent properties to materialize.

Externally, they can at times appear to have a confused thinking style. This is due to their ability to accept a broad range of information, much of which may be conflicting and needs processing. For this reason generative leaders have no problem in allowing contradictory situations or arguments to exist, they see them as part of an evaluative process rather than an end state. This can cause their colleagues some problems, particularly if they need more certainty and have a low tolerance for ambiguity.

This ability to operate in and explore ambiguous situations with little or no discomfort allows them to discover new relationships, ideas and, most importantly, new worlds. Their less tolerant colleagues, mode one, two, and three leaders, tend to react to ambiguity emotionally, creating for them "away from" conditions which usually result in actions being taken to reduce the ambiguity without exploring it properly and giving time for the emergent properties to surface and create an advantage.

Mode four and diversity

Generative leaders truly value diversity. For the mode four leader, diversity is the lifeblood of creativity and innovation. Forever on the lookout for different thinking and views, these leaders are tirelessly looking for challenges to their thinking and new approaches. They will often be found talking things over with a variety of people from all sorts of backgrounds and positions. They are like idea vacuum cleaners, constantly taking in views and arguments to test and develop their own thoughts. An outstanding attribute of a compound leader is their love of learning from any source. Unlike many other leaders, generative leaders will readily engage with, learn from, and, importantly, acknowledge anyone who contributes positively, regardless of position, age, experience, background, race, or any other distinguishing features. These are people who have no need to control, minimize others' contributions, or boost their own in others' eyes. People are important for their talent and the positive contribution they can make; rank, position, or qualifications are no guarantee of credibility to a mode four leader. Likewise, they are noticeable in that they will rarely pull rank or use devices such as higher qualifications, position, or experience to win arguments, instead logic, breadth of knowledge, and inspiration are the currency of mode four leaders.

Mode four relationships

The generative leader understands that influence and learning are dependent on functional relationships. As a result, these leaders are highly unlikely to allow any relationship to be degraded by positional conflict. Indeed, interpersonal conflict within the workplace with a mode four leader is rare; however, argument is not. These individuals work to keep good relationships with everyone even if they have professional disagreements with people. They see argument as a healthy and necessary part of the process of learning and creativity. Argument for the mode four leader is about testing ideas, exploring boundaries, and testing the validity and reliability of the assumptions on which the argument is based. There is no personal element to their argument and they are unlikely to personify an argument or take a stance based on power or aggression.

Generative vision

A striking feature of generative leaders is their strong vision of the future. They are by nature future-focused people, intent on creating the future they envision. This often involves a series of visions stretching out into the future, maybe 20 and 30 years ahead. These visions are not fixed in the minds of generative leaders; they are, to an extent, dynamic and will change as their learning develops. The visions that are closer in time tend to be more detailed and all compound leaders have a common trait in that they can see, hear, and feel the vision. Mode four leaders report that they have stepped into the vision of the future and experienced it through their own eyes, hear what will be happening, and feel what it will be like when they get to the future state they desire.

Further, they continually update the vision, and enroll others in it. This is done in a way which others describe as becoming caught up in the enthusiasm of the image of the future that such leaders paint.

The other side of the vision is the mode four leader's grasp of the reality of now; they know where they are starting from. This grasp on reality comes from the generative leader's obsession with learning. They have an insatiable and honest appetite for discovering how others perceive and understand their reality. From this they check and reference their own analysis of the current reality. Mode four leaders implicitly understand that reality is only a perception. This means they are well aware that they are likely to be not seeing something important. This results in a constant questioning and exploration in an attempt to find what they might be missing from any situation.

So knowing where they are starting from and where they are going to creates what Peter Senge refers to as "creative tension."[4] This is a driving and motivating force that places people in a constant creative problem-solving space as they move inexorably toward making their vision a new reality.

Generative buy-in and influence

The process by which mode four leaders capture others into their vision and ideas is by no means obvious. When examined initially, there appears to be no strategy and when questioned, the actual leaders are usually unable to articulate the process by which they manage to get others to enroll in and commit to a future which can often appear to others to be verging on science fiction.

The vision in 1976 of three men, 21-year-old Steve Jobs, 25-year-old Steve Wozniak, and Ronald G. Wayne, 41, working from a bedroom and then a garage, created Macintosh computers. This was a time when the only computers were large mainframes and there was no envisaged market for personal computers. Jobs and Wozniak took six months to complete their first work, a preassembled computer circuit board with no case, monitor, or keyboard and the mouse hadn't been invented yet. At this time, by selling these boards, both Steves were sharing an income of $250 a month. And yet their first business plan set a goal for sales to grow to $500 million in ten years. All this from a couple of young men operating from a garage who had to sell their VW van and Hewlett-Packard programmable calculator to raise $1,350 to finance production of the first boards.

The vision at the time – sales of $500 million for a product that had no established market and was predicted by others only likely to sell to a few university hobbyists – appeared to be somewhat fanciful. As it turned out, the company managed the target within five years. Further, their vision of an interactive user environment that didn't require programming knowledge, that anyone and everyone could use eventually gave rise to Apple OS in 1989, a very user-friendly interface. Other similar products began to emerge later for other computer types. All part of the vision that others thought a bit far-fetched!

The reality is that mode four leaders don't sell their vision. They engage others in the discussion to build the vision, their enthusiasm, and the richness of the future they paint becomes viral and spreads with increasing speed among the team.

A note about the nature of the modes of leadership

As will be expected, there are variations in each of the modes, as exemplified by individuals and their personality, background, and the situation or life conditions they currently perceive they exist in at any moment. It is also worth noting that individuals can move from one mode to another, depending on how they perceive their environment. So a mode three leader might start taking on mode one characteristics for a while if, for example, they believe it is needed to solve a problem. However, individuals will have a tendency toward one mode or another. Some individuals will remain in one mode all their life and others will progress toward mode four over time.

It is also important to recognize that individuals can be anywhere on the continuum from modal mode one to modal mode four – modal meaning that the individual will take on the majority of the attributes described in each mode. A leader can also be in transition between two modes or occupy a space between two conjoining modes, so, for example, taking on elements of both mode one and mode two attributes. In terms of distribution of modes in the general population, it would appear to be somewhat skewed towards mode two leadership. Mode one leaders accounted for approximately 31 percent of the research population, mode two accounts for approximately 55 percent and mode three 12.4 percent and mode four less than 1.6 percent (Figure 7.2).

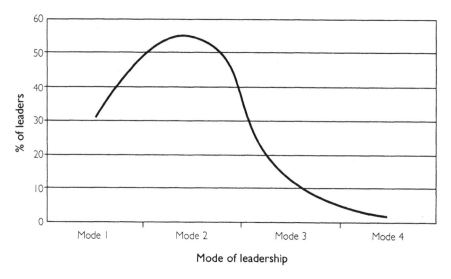

Figure 7.2 Approximate distribution of leadership modes

Problems that create change

Each mode has its own strengths and weaknesses, as described earlier, and in particular each mode has a set of problems that the leaders cannot solve, which are in essence created by the thinking system they are employing at the time. Mode one has a set of problems around control. The harder they try to control a situation, the more out of control things eventually become.[5] It is only when these leaders realize that trying to control natural processes or people has limited effects that there is a recognition that the very tools of hegemony that they are using are actually the cause of the wild variations experienced.[6] Once they give up trying to manipulate their environment and others, things start to settle down. It is at this moment that there is usually a realization that cooperative thinking, values, and behaviors will provide the solutions which had previously eluded them.

Thus starts the transition to mode two thinking and a leadership style that is more cooperative in nature. This is because people are now seen as valuable resources that can help a mode two leader achieve their aims. The problem for mode two thinkers is that while cooperation is an ideal, the very difference in people's values, beliefs, and goals creates conflict. So mode two leaders, realizing that control doesn't get the best out of their staff or the situations they find themselves in, turn toward promoting cooperation, in the hope that working together with their team will make the best of the resources available and help them to solve the problems of the wild deviations experienced before. Certainly this happens as the staff of the new mode two leader start to feel more appreciated and valued. The differences between people that were repressed before now start to surface and cause conflict.

As the mode two leader progresses toward modal mode two, they redouble their efforts to gain cooperation and reduce the conflict. This can take a number of forms. If the leader sees the conflict as a failure and becomes defensive, especially where the conflict has become noticeable outside the team, the leader can revert back to mode one control to stop the conflict, which is an emotional response. However, if the leader is committed to either staying away from the wild fluctuations experienced before or going toward a more cooperative process, they will redouble their efforts and eventually appeal to people's better nature, often by engaging external help, usually in the form of consultants, to carry out team building that usually works to some extent. However, eventually the cooperative style fails to deliver the agreements required for peak performance, which includes trying to get the cooperation of internal individuals, teams and departments, and external customers and suppliers as well as other companies. This is largely due to their efforts to control the situation more covertly through what is ostensively manipulation.

As they move toward the transition with mode three, there is an awareness that trying to gain cooperation when people's goals, values, and beliefs aren't aligned is never going to work. It is at this point that their thoughts turn toward changing mindsets and aligning values. The transition to mode three is marked by increasing calls for true consensus and not merely cooperation. This is achieved usually by genuine debate and thrashing things out. Values become part of the battleground for hearts and minds.

As the leader moves into a modal mode three position, winning people over, influencing thinking, and innovation become the aims. The big problem with this is that consensus, especially at a values level, takes time. Mode three teams are big on ideas and discussion and conversely low on action. A lot of effort is spent gaining a single shared vision. When problem solving, mode three teams will tend toward adaptive solutions and will work hard at gaining deep buy-in to those solutions that are ecological to all concerned, including the employees, the company, and the environment. The problem that mode three leaders face is that this takes time and productivity suffers as projects get drawn out. As time and productivity become the problem that haunts mode three leaders, the next transition is a total shift in thinking.

The progression from mode three to four, rather than an evolutionary step like the previous transitions, is nothing short of revolution. Mode four leaders can be seen by others as cheats. These are the people who write and rewrite the rules to suit the situation. Hugely pragmatic, mode four leaders are polychronic, work incredibly fast, and do not fear mistakes. Their whole orientation is toward learning. They pick up new ideas quickly, try them, and if they don't work, dump them without ceremony. The solutions they tend toward are more generative in nature, creating new realities and finding new opportunities in situations that others are struggling just to control. They are flexible to the point that they will go after an opportunity to explore its potential and then move on. These are people who, if not in a formal leadership role, are hard if not impossible to manage. Frequently seen as mavericks, their quest is for freedom – freedom to explore without constraint. These are true entrepreneurs who experiment and play with ideas to see what will happen, to discover which idea will give them the advantage. As a result, where others will scorn what they see as a line of failures, the mode four leader will see it as useful learning to build on and learn even faster on the road to success. The loyalty a generative individual feels is only to the generation of ideas and opportunities. They operate comfortably in situations of high ambiguity. Indeed, as one moves up the modes, there is an increase in flexibility, the ability to discern and tolerate ambiguity until the transition (that few make) into mode four. At this level, it is no longer an issue of tolerance of ambiguity, instead one of an expectation of and a desire for complexity and ambiguity. This is where the big rewards are.[7]

When presenting this material, a question I am often asked is how can you change people to attain higher leadership modality. This question in itself comes from a control orientation and is typical of mode two and three thinking. The idea of changing someone else presupposes that there is a direct causal relationship between an action that they will take and the effect, some predictable reaction or change in another person. A mode four leader is more likely to ask what opportunities exist in the distribution of modalities in their organization and they will wonder what can happen so that they can take advantage from such a mix, the emergent properties of diversity.

Each mode of leadership has its own strengths and weaknesses. That said, certain leadership modes lend themselves to the type of problem being experienced at any given point in time. It would also appear to hold that each leadership mode is most likely to see a presenting problem of the type associated with their mode. So, for example, a mode one leader will perceive each problem they encounter as a technical one. In addition, they may not even notice a type III or IV problem. If they do notice such a problem, they are most likely to reduce it to a type I technical problem and apply type I solutions, usually with limited results.

Likewise, mode two leaders will tend to notice type II problems; however, they are quite able to recognize and solve a type I problem as well. Thus a leader will have a tendency to notice and therefore fit the presenting problem or issue into the problem type associated with their modality. However, they do have the ability to diagnose and solve lower problem types but will first defer to the problem type associated with their mode of leadership. Thus mode four leaders have the widest range of latitude for problem solving, being able to apply all four problem type solutions. It is unlikely that any other mode will notice or correctly diagnose problem types associated with higher leadership modalities.

While mode four leaders have the ability to recognize and solve, say, a type I technical problem, they are unlikely to invest much time or energy in such an endeavor as their preference will be toward type IV generative problems. So while they are capable of solving a type I problem, they may not be the person best suited to ensuring a quality solution in that context. They do, for example, have a tendency to reframe problems before fully exploring other solution types.

Another thing to make note of at this juncture is that the higher the problem type (toward type IV), the more complexity and ambiguity there is. Mode four leaders are the most well equipped to deal with highly ambiguous situations, which tend to be new world and future-paced situations. They are not good in situations where slow incremental change is required, where type I problems abound, situations such as maintaining or fine-tuning a system. Such situations suit mode one and two leaders far better.

Freedom vs security

The orientation of generative leaders is freedom. The orientation of technical leaders is security. Mode one individuals are risk-averse, whereas mode four leaders will take, what to some, particularly those of the lower modalities, appear to be stupid risks – risks that from the perspective of mode one and two leaders may well appear to be career-limiting. They can be seen to go where angels fear to tread. The generative leaders' subtext is a drive toward freedom, to cast away what they see as the shackles inherent in all organizations and bureaucratic systems, for instance systems set up by the state for car registration, tax and so on, which all annoy the mode four individual. One of the reasons why there are so few mode four individuals in organizations is somewhat of a dichotomy. While on the one hand, these are the masters of ambiguity, on the other they often find it difficult to cope with systems and bureaucracy, sometimes to the extent that their search for freedom will cause them to leave or try to leave the structure of the organization, and in some cases their country, in an attempt to get away from the things that they see as preventing their freedom. This then is the problem that mode four leaders can't solve; how to have freedom and at the same time accept the bureaucracy and structure that exists in all worlds. This means that there is a mode above mode four; however, at the moment, the research evidence is somewhat sketchy, mainly because finding individuals in this mode is difficult on two counts. First, there are so few of them and second, individuals who are mode five are likely to have left organizations and other structured work environments on which this research was based. The next phase of this work is, at the time of writing, currently ongoing to find and describe mode five individuals.

Context or trait?

The question is whether the modes of leadership are brought about due to the context individuals find themselves in, or because of some set of traits inherent in their personality.

The answer appears to be yes to both. There is good evidence that to a certain extent an individual will use different strategies in different contexts *depending* on the level of ambiguity they experience and the intensity of stress/threat they perceive as a result. The greater the stress, the more prone an individual will be to reverting to their base response, which is the modality that they are most comfortable in, which is defined by their personality.

Some individuals, it would appear, stay in one mode of leadership all their working lives. Others will move and transition, each to their own level and with individual and unique attributes of those levels, showing that the context is not the only driver for change.

Conclusion

The picture painted here of the four modes of leadership strongly suggests that within any organization the key to success is the ability to manage the diversity of leadership encountered. Situations where slow incremental change or stability and direction is required would most likely suit mode one leaders.

Where a more cooperative yet steady approach is required where, for example, it is important to get things right and for teams to follow procedures, then a mode two leadership stance would be ideal.

In situations where relationships are key and the generation of ideas as important as harmony, then a mode three approach would work best.

If, on the other hand, disruptive innovation and change is needed or there is a requirement for new thinking and futuristic solutions, a mode four leader would be best suited.

Placing any individual in the wrong context for too long will cause stress for the leader and those around them, unless of course the situation becomes a catalyst for change in the leader's approach and thinking.

A number of organizations, like Honda for example, now actively manage such diversity, engaging in active talent management to place individuals in the situation that will employ them most profitably. Mode one leaders being placed in the most technical areas and mode four individuals leading in the future pacing elements of the business, for example.

This gives rise to a new way of constructing organizations based on the talent of the diversity of the individuals and teams available. A different way of looking at teams and their leadership and how to gain the advantage from ambiguity.

Part III
Finding the Advantage

If you think that ambiguity is ambiguous you should try getting people to work with it, then you will enter into a whole new world where the usual training and development "think" gets turned on its head. David Wilkinson

The final part of this volume aims to help individuals learn the secrets and skills of mode four leaders, those most able to deal profitably with highly ambiguous situations, bordering on or entering states of chaos. Chapter 8 is a synopsis of the research findings drawn from observations of those who lead in such situations or more often rise to prominence in times of emergency with their new logic and persuasive arguments, usually in vacuous leadership conditions.

The 11 lessons contained in this chapter give an insight into the workings of a world of constant change and innovation, where possibilities abound and new futures beckon.

Chapter 9 briefly examines some tools for creative problem solving that are frequently used when the current solutions either don't work or are not innovative enough.

Chapter 10, Developing Ambiguity Acuity, explores a variety of techniques that individuals can use to help to increase their own and others' tolerance to ambiguity.

Getting people to develop while in an ambiguous situation is difficult. Usually time spent preparing individuals and teams, working on the thinking, skills, and understanding of their own and others' emotions in ambiguous situations is an investment with potentially high returns. In terms of disaster management, such preparation is vital, as shown by incidents like the U.S. response to hurricane Katrina. It saves lives. In less life-threatening contexts, it can mean the difference between profit and loss, survival and oblivion, or being constrained by the past and being able to construct and lead our own futures.

Imagination is more important than knowledge. **Albert Einstein, German mathematical physicist (1879–1955)**

In this chapter we explore the attributes of effective generative leaders that positively contribute to their success in solving problems in ambiguous situations and that allow them to gain the advantage. These lessons include:

1 Knowing the difference between problem types and hence being able to identify current levels of risk, uncertainty, vagueness, or ambiguity to solve problems.

2 Understanding the difference between learning and decision-making orientations and knowing which situations to use when.

3 Setting detailed goals and yet leaving the route to achieving them open.

4 Using high levels of emotional intelligence.

5 Seeking out diversity and challenge.

6 Being an incurable and incorrigible learner.

7 Searching for risk, uncertainty, and ambiguity – the places where the highest rewards are.

8 Being able to correctly analyze the different problem types and solve each type.

9 Being a generative communicator.

10 Understanding how to use pull influence and networks to explore ambiguity and create new worlds for others to walk into.

11 The only rules are useful rules.

Good leaders identify ambiguity and don't flee from it or fight it. They stay with ambiguity, explore it for possibilities, discover decisions, and are comfortable altering those decisions and making new decisions in the light of new information and/or new thinking, while positively influencing the thinking and actions of others. In short, they look on ambiguity as an opportunity to learn.

The world of disaster management is a good illustration here. We train disaster managers to be highly flexible and not depend on standard operating procedures or disaster plans for defining their actions. Instead they use the plans as a starting guide, constantly evaluating where and when they are working. It is rare for a disaster to happen in just the way the planners predicted. The armed forces have a saying that all plans are good until first contact with the enemy. In a disaster, ambiguity is high because in the first moments of a disaster, knowledge is usually very low. A good disaster manager will use the plans as a guide and start to take action to generate knowledge, being aware that things may not be as they currently think they are and open to changing their course of action as their knowledge increases. Their decisions are based on their learning of the new world and not the rules and order of the old world, unless of course they apply.

Further, they use planning as a process of learning rather than of trying to lay down dictates. Planning is a vital part of the mental preparation for incidents, playing out and imagining scenarios. The important part of developing a plan isn't so much the actual plan, although it has its place, it is more the learning and the creative and imaginative processes that devising such a plan usefully exercises, which is why plans prepared for others to follow frequently succeed in their inception and fail in their implementation. The U.K. military use the planning process to help them define and refine the purpose of the mission and not merely the process. This means that everyone understands what the objective of their mission is and they are trained to achieve that purpose even if the tasks that were originally planned no longer have currency in the situation.

An analysis of failures in disaster situations, such as during hurricane Katrina, can be tracked to either unclear or outdated purpose definitions or task fixation, in other words, a singular lack of flexibility or tolerance to ambiguity on behalf of those leading, carrying out, or managing the implementation of the plan. Successes in situations of ambiguity tend to be down to two factors; first, a clear purpose or problem definition gained through prior creative and imaginative visions or scenario building as well as problem definition testing. Second, on tolerance of ambiguity or, preferably, enjoyable and creative exploration of the degrees of freedom that ambiguous situations offer. There are a series of underlying attributes which help with the ability to deal creatively with ambiguity and exploit the advantages and emergent properties inherent in such situations.

Having discussed the nature of ambiguity and the modes of leadership, I have alluded to the attributes that make mode four leaders so good at creating advantage from ambiguity, the very conditions from which other leaders try to escape or move away. The following 11 lessons have been extracted from observations of successful leaders in ambiguous situations.

Lesson I

"We still have a problem with the appraisal scheme."

"I know, we just need to make them all do it somehow."

"Well I suggest that we look at the appraisal forms again. A new scheme, that's what we need."

"Yes but we need a policy that makes people complete the appraisal."

The company concerned had a centralized annual appraisal scheme. This had been devised some years before and was administered by the institution's HR department. The scheme was a standard process involving the requirement for managers to have an interview with their staff on an individual basis, reviewing the past year's achievements and work, giving evidence of performance and setting goals for the future, together with identifying any development needs the member of staff might have. Managers are then required to complete a number of forms. One is returned to the HR department to confirm that the appraisal interview has been completed, a copy of the actual appraisal notes is kept by the manager and another copy is given to the member of staff with their performance targets. Lastly, a form is sent to the training and development department with any development needs the individual has for the coming year.

However, in reality, the scheme had largely fallen into disuse, with less than 30 percent of the company returning the forms. The HR function had tried on a number of occasions to reinvigorate the scheme, holding regular training events and sending a series of memos and letters of advice to managers and staff about the importance of the scheme, with little discernable effect. The latest attempt involved changing the paperwork to give the scheme more options because it was felt that the various grades of staff had different requirements. Again this did not entice any more managers and staff to use the scheme. The problem was being seen as a technical one by the HR function; change the forms, change the letter, until finally a policy document was produced, stating that "managers will carry out appraisal meetings once a year with their staff." This mode one solution went largely unnoticed in the plethora of policy documents created by the department and so had no measurable impact.

The HR department concerned was currently engaged in yet another revision of the paperwork when one of the heads of department was asked for her ideas. Her first response was to go and talk to some managers. She found that about 40 percent of the managers weren't holding appraisal interviews of any type and 30 percent were holding a wide variety of appraisal "events" but weren't using the official forms or processes. The remaining 30 percent of managers were using the official scheme and forms. She also discovered a variety of reasons for the lack of use of the scheme, including having no career pathway (cleaners and people in closed job systems), "it's just a paper exercise," "nothing ever happens with the appraisal," and "what's the point, my manager doesn't really know what I do." Unlike the others, this particular department head realized that she was not dealing with a technical problem, that the problem was not an administrative one, but that a large number of managers and staff were not taking their responsibilities seriously, and some staff were not exercising their right to an appraisal or feedback from their managers. The solution to this problem, she realized, required either the cooperation of the managers and staff, or the company had to adapt to the situation and redefine the problem. The problem was not that some forms were not being filled in. The problem was not even that appraisal interviews were not being carried out. The problem was twofold: first, some managers were not taking their managerial duties seriously, ensuring that their staff were performing effectively and supporting them by ensuring that they had what they needed to be able to do their jobs effectively and safely. Second, staff had no incentive or reason to do an appraisal – nothing happened as a result of it. This, she reasoned, required managers to have contact with their staff and understand how they were performing, what their problems were and to ensure their safety, including psychological aspects of their safety. This meant that the problem was to re-engage those managers who were disengaged from their staff and get them to build relationships with them, so that they started to take on the responsibilities they were being paid for. Her solution to the problem was different to the problem the rest of her colleagues were working on.

Generative leaders understand the difference between risk, uncertainty, vagueness, and ambiguity and are able to operate with all four. These leaders can identify the level of the situation, from the nature of the problem they are facing, be it a technical, cooperative, adaptive, or generative problem (see lesson 8). This in turn means that the individual can define problems accurately – in this case moving the problem from a technical issue and turning it into a collaborative one.

Lesson 2

Compound leaders know the difference between learning and decision-making orientations and when to use each, utilizing a triage process based on urgency and importance. Consider the following two scenarios.

John Anstey called order and glanced around the table at the worried-looking faces. "This is a serious situation and I am not going to beat about the bush. I have just heard that Arnoid has gone into receivership this morning without warning. As you know, in terms of capital sales they were our largest customer, with orders this year exceeding $800,000 or 65 percent of our sales this year to date. The sudden cancellation of the Arnoid order means that we are left with about $500,000 of stock that was due to be delivered tomorrow, which is on account. The bottom line is this. If we don't shift this stock and soon, we are going to be in serious difficulties. Unfortunately, as you will know, this has hit us just after we made the investment in the new plant and are currently in a negative equity situation. The fulfillment of this order was supposed to pay for the new production plant. OK, I want us to stay calm and get thinking. This is just a problem like any other and problems can be solved. This is also a situation with potential, if handled right we should be in a stronger position after this. So let's see what we can learn and what we can create from this. I will be staying here until we have got this licked. The first ideas meeting will take place at four this afternoon. We will meet at nine and four every day until we understand the problem properly, the opportunities available and have a range of solutions, but let's see what the problem really is first. So let's go to it. I'll see you all at four with your thoughts about what problem we should be solving and what opportunities this situation presents."

"OK, listen up folks. We have a problem. The third stage production unit has just broken down. Jim, I want you to go to the plant and make sure that the engineers have what they need to get this sorted and keep me informed. Shirley, go to the first stage plant and John to the second stage plant and manage production between you so that we don't lose any material and ensure they are ready to go once the third stage plant is up and running. Alex, I want you to manage the post-third stages so they are also ready once the third is going again. Hillary, I need you to coordinate the communications between the rest of the team. The principle here is to reduce wastage and downtime. This might also be a good time for the idle to do some maintenance as long as it can be returned to operational status when we need it. James, I want you to look around and explore how we can take advantage from situations like this. OK, let's go!"

In the first example, the leader realized that this was a time for learning and discovery of opportunity. The leader concerned didn't try to control or direct. While the situation was important and reasonably urgent, hence the emphasis on time and regular meetings to build a sense of urgency, this was not yet a situation with critical urgency. The leader prioritized creativity and problem definition and did not allow any negative emotional reactions to the situation to force him into a panicked response for a solution before really understanding how else the problem might be expressed and what the nature of the problem might be. Well, you might argue, the problem is obvious, isn't it? The company's major client has gone bust, leaving the company with a huge unsold stock and in a deficit position. Not so. In reality, later that day the team came back, having generated a series of over 300 problem options (new problem definitions) including:

■ What new clients can we find to sell the stock to?

■ How can we find new clients?

■ What new sectors are we not now exploring?

■ How might we change the way we charge for our products?

■ How might we increase the diversity of our sales base to spread risk?

■ How might we change the way we deliver products to decrease the time from production to delivery?

■ In what ways might we reduce stock holdings?

■ How can we insure against such possibilities?

■ How might we collaborate with our competitors to reduce our current stock holdings and keep or increase the profit margin on the production?

■ How might we sell the stock direct to the end user?

■ How might we disassemble, modify or change the stock to find a new market?

As you can imagine from the nature of the questions above, the mood in the room had changed from fear and negative problem solving (trying to move away from or get out of a situation) into a stimulating, positive problem set, which was moving toward an exciting new future and into a positive new world. The change in the atmosphere and energy in the room had shifted significantly since the announcement. There was now a growing air of excited expectancy and total focus. This no longer looked like a company in crisis but a dynamic business about to turn a problem into a real advantage. In the end, it forced two of its competitors out of business and saw its profits leap over 45 percent within a year. This leader understood when to use a primarily explorative learning orientation.

In the second scenario, the leader realized that this situation was important and had critical urgency. So she took control, stopping other noncritical work, directing the managers to manage on the ground while the situation persisted. You will have noted that one manager was tasked to keep an overview and ensure good communications and another was required to roam and find what he could learn from the situation that might present some opportunities. This uncovered the fact that one of the processes in one of the plants had been changed by the operators without anyone realizing – a sort of shortcut. When explored without judgment, it was found that this shortcut meant that the process could operate with one less person without any change in efficiency or safety. An individual was reassigned to another part of the factory where there had been a long period of staff shortage.

Once the situation had been resolved, the leader then held a debrief with her managers who had each debriefed their teams. The debrief had a very particular format. All the staff and then the managers were asked to come up with as many answers as they could to two questions. What have we learnt from this? What would you advise happens next time? This pyramid of learning provided such a rich vein of wisdom that a number of changes were made that improved production slightly and the company's ability to respond to critical incidents significantly. Again, during the entire situation, what could easily have created a domino effect of negative energy, emotions, and stress responses was turned into a positive experience for almost everyone and left a sense excitement and enthusiasm in the company. Incidentally, an emergent property of the way the situation was handled was that staff turnover in the company fell from

17 percent to just over 8 percent for the following nine months, with the additional benefit of a substantial saving in recruitment and training costs for the period. This leader knew when to take a primarily decision-making orientation to the problem, although it has to be noted that she couldn't help herself from trying to tag at least some learning orientation into the situation – the debriefings were wholly about learning and everyone was involved.

Knowing when to apply a learning orientation and when to make decisions is crucial to great leadership and particularly working with ambiguity.

Lesson 3

Against conventional wisdom, mode four leaders set goals or purpose but don't specify the precise route to achieve them, preferring to remain flexible.

Generative leaders are big on vision. They set goals that they create as a living vision, they can see what it will be like when it has been achieved, they can hear what will be being said when the goal is in place. They know what it will feel like when they have arrived. The goal is very specific; they don't say, I want to make lots of money. They say, I will make $200,000 by January 31 next year. They then visualize it having happened, what will be happening around them and how things will appear when it has happened. The vision is very specific.

Now, at this point, they start to vary from the conventional wisdom which states that you need to draw up a detailed step-by-step plan of how to get there. Generative leaders don't appear to do this. They have an idea how they might achieve the goal, but it is little more that that. What they do instead of having a detailed plan is start looking for doors that they can open that will move them toward the goal. When you have a strong and compelling goal, everything suddenly becomes a potential opportunity for moving toward or achieving that goal. These are opportunities that others often miss. The following is a good example of this in action.

A departmental leader in a company had a compelling vision of moving his department's function into the international market. Until now the company had only traded within New Zealand. He and his team created a solid vision that included international travel. The first opportunity that came his way was that the board asked each departmental head for a business plan for the next two years. He included part of the vision about breaking into international markets. His immediate manager sent the plan back with a note, "Brett, I think you should remove the reference to making sales in other countries. It's just not in the company's strategic plan." Brett kept it in and sent it to the board.

Nothing happened for many months. No one had appeared to notice the reference and nothing was said about the business plan, until one day seven months later when his manager came to see him.

"Brett, the operations director has asked to see you. I don't know what it is about, but you'd better get up there."

When Brett arrived, the operations director, a stern man of about 55, with a shock of white hair, sat him down and offered him a cup of coffee.

"Brett, I have called you here because some months ago now you wrote something in your business plan about moving into the international market. I am sorry that it's taken me so long to get back to you. First, I wanted you to know that we had read your plan. Second, I was going to tell you that we have no plans for such a move."

Brett slumped in the chair.

"Indeed, just a week ago, I would have said the same thing to you. However, yesterday we were approached by a company from Japan that is interested in what we are doing. We are not so sure that this is where we want to go but we agreed to a meeting anyway. The thing is Brett, I would like you to come to the meeting to get your opinion on their proposal. I am particularly interested in finding out from you how, if we were to go ahead with this, it would affect departments like yours. As you expressed an interest in this sort of thing, I thought you would at least give the proposal a fair hearing."

The meeting in Wellington was followed by another in Asaki, where, during a social event, Brett started to talk to another business man from a different company and saw a further opening for the services of his company and his vision. The company came away with two substantial contracts and Brett and his team were placed in charge of one of the projects. This led to a number of other contacts around the Pacific Rim, because every time Brett or a member of his team met someone or visited anywhere, their focus was on creating international trade. Now it could be argued that the first opportunity was luck, however, Brett had created the luck and then went on to spot opportunities everywhere he went. Not all of them paid off but, on average, Brett and his team landed one large contract every 16 months. Today, Brett heads up the company's overseas division with offices in six different countries.

Lesson 4

Generative leaders have a high level of emotional intelligence. They have the ability to recognize their own feelings and those of others, they can easily inspire and enthuse themselves and others by managing their own and others' emotions. Essentially, there are four elements which constitute emotional intelligence:[1]

- *Emotional perception and identification* – the ability to accurately identify emotions in oneself and others in a wide variety of contexts through people's body language, the words they use, the intonation of their voice, for example in stories and music.

- *Emotional facilitation of thought* – the ability to be able to use emotions to help one to think and solve problems. Basically, this is the ability to integrate emotions into one's thinking.

- *Emotional understanding* – this is the ability to be able to recognize, analyze, and solve emotional problems, both in oneself and others.

- *Emotional management* – the ability to regulate and control emotions in yourself, manage other people's emotional states, and being able to understand the consequences of social acts on others.

It should be noted that these four elements implicitly imply not only the ability and the capacity to learn and develop one's thinking and actions in each of these four areas, but also an unceasing and insatiable appetite for such learning on a continual basis.

Let's look at an extreme example from the month that followed the Southeast Asia tsunami disaster in 2004.

There was a group of managers running a relief center on an island which had been devastated by the earthquake and resultant wave. Bodies were still being recovered at this stage. As can be imagined, this is a gruesome and stressful task at the best of times, but after weeks in the searing heat and with the corrosive effects of the salt water, predators and so on, the task had become a nightmare situation.

The task was not just to find and bury the bodies but also, if possible, to identify them by whatever means necessary. By this time, fingerprints were largely a forlorn hope and photographs, while taken, were virtually useless. There was some DNA capability but the kits were in short supply. These tasks were being carried out in the most rudimentary conditions imaginable, as almost all of the lines of communication and power had been wiped out.

Added to this was the problem that the survivors were also looking for loved ones, in the hope that they would at least know what had happened to them and could give them the decency of a dignified ceremony, according to local and religious customs. This was a chaotic, stressful, and distressing time for those tasked with the post-disaster relief work. Lives were still being lost even after this length of time, largely from injuries and infections.

During one such operation, a group of about 13 bodies had been discovered in a remote area under some debris caught up in some trees at the edge of a forest. Two inexperienced members of the team arrived and radioed back, confirming the gruesome find and requesting some help. Both were shaken and were reacting badly to the find. Neither had ever seen bodies in such a state, and since they had arrived they had never been in any similar situation without a supervisor or a more experienced team member with them.

While they were waiting for the team, a group of about 15 local people, who had seen the arrival of the two scouts, arrived in boats. They wanted to check the bodies to see if they were members of their village. Apart from the fact that by now the bodies were unrecognizable and in a fragile condition, there was also a serious risk of infection from handling them. However, the two shaken scouts had let the people go up to the bodies.

The rest of the team arrived to find that there was by now a very distressed group of villagers and two traumatized scouts. The team leader approached and shouted at the scouts, "What the hell is going on, you idiots. Why have you let them go anywhere near that lot. Are you stupid or something? I'll see you two when we get back." As a punishment, they were made to remove the villagers by force and then the bodies with little help of the rest of the team.

Compare this with another team in another part of the same area where the leader ensured that all novice team members were always with more experienced staff, that he fully briefed every member of the team before and after any operation. He openly talked about his emotions and reactions to the situation and invited others to do the same. Furthermore, he tried where possible to ensure that members of his team were cycled between those jobs which were likely to be more distressing and the administrative tasks which needed to be undertaken. Also, he trained every member of his team so that they could identify the symptoms of traumatic stress disorder, both in themselves and others.

Lesson 5

Generative leaders actively look for and genuinely value difference and diversity in people. Unlike leaders of the other modalities, mode four leaders recruit diverse teams and look for the differences in individuals. The rationale they use is that in problem solving, it is different thinking that, if listened to without prejudgment, may just yield or lead to the solution that works. Additionally, they reason that different perspectives on issues test your own thinking and they welcome this. These are not defensive people, their orientation is learning, not trying to defend their own views, they are only interested in making things work, they are committed to the most pragmatic approach to achieve their goals, which are usually future paced.

For these leaders, diversity isn't a set of politically correct actions to satisfy some external pressure, diversity is about diversity of thinking. The generative leader equates diversity of thinking with the ability to recognize and accept new things, ideas, and situations. They fully recognize the limiting danger inherent in prejudging any person, idea or situation without first exploring the new proposal and evaluating its validity in the situation and, in particular, the opportunities that the new person, idea or situation presents. These leaders hate to miss an opening.

Furthermore, mode four leaders are aware of the restrictive

hazards that working with people who all think alike occasions. While the other types of leaders feel more comfortable with people who think and behave like they do, and prefer agreement to their ideas rather than the challenge of different thoughts and practices, mode four leaders prefer the reality check of different perspectives even if it is uncomfortable.

Teams that have been recruited for their similarity in outlook can be found in almost every organization in the world and people who stand out and are considered to be different or odd are often sidelined or even removed either overtly or covertly by a process of constructive dismissal. These are the very people who mode four leaders seek and engage with. They recognize the competitive and innovative advantage in thinking differently; these are the leaders who truly value diversity.

This is a process that has become known as "broadbanding," which is the opposite of "narrowband thinking." Narrowband thinkers take in only focused information that collaborates with their view of the world. They delete, distort, and generalize incoming data so that it can fit into their narrowband view of the world. Broadband thinkers, on the other hand, can take in a wide diversity of often conflicting data, exploring, learning, and looking for opportunities from them (see Figure 8.1).

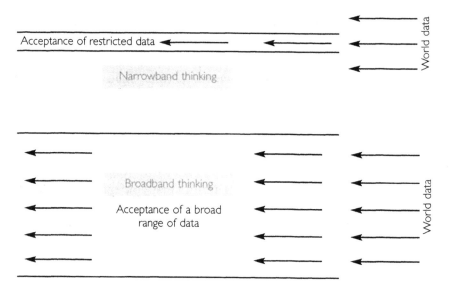

Figure 8.1 Narrowband thinking and broadbanding

Lesson 6

Great leaders all have a strong learning orientation; they are inquisitive and have a tendency toward questions rather than statements and opinions. For example, when faced with a situation that is ambiguous or uncertain, they are the least likely leaders to feel the need to show that they know what is happening by giving their opinion or making statements about the situation. They are, however, the most likely to lead the way by exploring the situation and asking questions. They will often ask the questions that on the surface sometimes appear to be daft questions, however, it is these very questions that often identify the hidden assumptions that ideas and propositions are based on.

So what is the key to the mode four leaders' ability to learn so readily from new situations? It would appear that generative leaders, unlike other modes of leaders, are unlikely to prejudge new information, situations, or people, regardless of how odd they may appear to others. Also, unlike other professionals, generative leaders continue to learn as they mature and the rate of their learning increases over time. At no time do they think that they know enough or that they are beyond learning from others, regardless of the other's situation or position.

Lesson 7

Great leaders look for ambiguity, uncertainty, and risk. They know that the greatest rewards exist where there is risk, new learning will be found where there is uncertainty, and exploration of ambiguity is likely to reveal new worlds. Unlike other leaders, these people are not only quite comfortable with risk, uncertainty, vagueness, and ambiguity, but actually seek it out. The indicators they look for are where others are having problems, are stressed, or in denial. They then move in and start exploring, which, together with their open learning orientation based on a lack of prejudgment, makes them ideally suited for discovering the advantages available in such situations.

Lesson 8

Mode four leaders can solve all problem types. In addition, they are creationists and have the capacity to solve generative problems. The four problem types are now discussed in detail.

Type I problems

Type I problems are *technical problems*. These are the sort of problems where a specialist, for example a car mechanic or a doctor, follows a prescribed route to solve a problem. In the case of a car mechanic, they will follow a diagnostic route depending on the symptoms presented. To solve the problem, they will apply a tried and tested problem-solving path that is laid down prescribing the technical solution. Such problems can be mapped out using decision trees. So the mechanic will diagnose that the fuel filter needs to be replaced and does so to solve the problem. The doctor who prescribes a medicine which clears up an illness is also engaging in type I problem solving.

The level of creativity required for the solution of such problems is relatively low. As long as the specialist has the knowledge of the process required to correctly diagnose the problem, the solution is usually prescribed. Mode one leaders are largely restricted to type I solutions, regardless of the type of problem they encounter, frequently forcing technical solutions on more complex problem types.

Type II problems

Type II problems are those predicaments that require a *cooperative* solution. For example, a mechanic will say, "Look, I can fix the engine, but if you keep putting the wrong fuel in the tank, it will keep breaking down. You need to start using the correct fuel." Similarly, the doctor who prescribes some medicine and states, "You need to lose some weight or this problem is going to get worse." Both problems require some level of cooperation as part of the solution. Mode two leaders will often interpret problems as type II problems and will call for some form of cooperative solution. They can, however, solve type I problems if the solution is within their technical knowledge and experience.

Type III problems

Type III problems, also known as *adaptive problems,* require some form of adaptation to solve and move forward. So, for example, the mechanic diagnoses that the engine is beyond repair and the customer now has to adapt to the situation – they either have to walk, have a new engine fitted, or buy a new car. The medical analogy would be where someone was diagnosed with an incurable condition. They are going to have to adapt to the situation and come to terms with it to move forward.

Type IV problems

Type IV problems are also known as *generative* or *creationist problems* and are of an entirely different order to any previously mentioned. Each of the previous problem types means that a problem has occurred and has been recognized. This sounds like it is stating the blindingly obvious; however, it also means that certain conditions have to be true for such problems to exist.

The first is that the problem has to occur before it is recognized. This means that there is usually a time lag between the problem occurring and the recognition of the problem. If the problem is not too complex, the time lag between the problem occurring and its recognition is short, and the problem type is diagnosed correctly, then the problem may well be solved. However, the issue here is that the energy is going into solving a historical problem, it is in effect negative energy being spent to bring things back to normal. In effect, if you have a problem, you have a problem. The longer the time between the problem occurring and its correct diagnosis, the more energy it will require to solve and bring back to the original state (see Figure 7.1).

The second condition is that type I problems are rule-based problems and type II and III problem solving involves what is known as CBR or case-based reasoning. CBR is a form of logical problem solving that is dependent on the person's or the team's memory of previous cases or problem solutions that are identifiably similar to the problem case under consideration. They have to apply the rules, or the historical case, or a combination of cases to the current problem. This is a sort of pick and mix building of solutions from an experimental database.

Unlike the previous three problem-solving types, type IV problem solving moves into the future. This is predictive problem solving and is largely the province of generative leaders. One of the most famous type IV generative solutions is the Mont Fleur scenario,[2] which was used by Shell Oil in South Africa to help the country in the transition from the apartheid regime to a fully democratic government. The first part of the process was for Shell to engage in a generative problem-solving process in which they created over 30 possible future scenarios for the country. These were condensed first into 12 and finally to four pictures of the possible futures. The first scenario was called the "ostrich" scenario, in which the minority white government led by F.W. de Klerk stuck its head in the sand and caused a protracted and non-negotiated process to occur, which made any democratic and representative handover of power almost impossible without further bloodshed. The second setting was called the "lame duck" scenario in which the various factions of a new government descend into such a weakened state that it cannot govern adequately. The third story, "Icarus," painted a picture whereby a new black government was swept into power on a wave of popular fervor and idealism, which caused the new government to bust the economy in a wave of unsustainable growth. The last scenario, named the "flight of the flamingos," set out a scene in which the transition of power was smooth and all the precursors to a successful, economically viable change of rule were put into place.

They then published a booklet outlining the scenarios in the popular press, distributed a cartoon video of the scenarios and ran over 100 workshops with leaders from many factions about the settings. These actions placed the vocabulary of the scenarios into popular language and de Klerk responded by stating that he was not an ostrich. The generative nature of the problem solving used in the Mont Fleur process is widely credited with creating the conditions through which the transition of power was a smooth and productive process and did not descend into chaos.

Lesson 9

Mode four leaders engage in generative discourse. There are four categories of discursive behaviors:[3]

■ *Downloading.* The assumption made here is that people download what we say as we meant it to be said. When we are talking with this model of communication in mind, we have a script and run the script regardless of the context, or the situation that the other person or people are in. People in this mode will keep talking and are unlikely to notice the cues from others that they are not listening.

■ *Debating.* This is where when others are talking, we are either thinking about how we are going to respond, mentally building up arguments, or storing lines of reasoning to reply with. It is often called pseudo-listening, where we pretend to listen, giving off all the nonverbal signals while being otherwise engaged inside. The behaviors typical of debating include defending our own arguments even in the face of evidence to the contrary, sleights of mouth, and spin. The aim in this category of communication is usually to win.

■ *Active.* This happens when we listen with empathy and try to get inside the person we are listening to and understand their point of view and how they are seeing things, without prejudgment. It is hard for most people to quiet the voices of judgment and rationale.

Most texts end at this point, however, there is one further type of listening that is based on, but transcends, active or empathetic listening.

■ *Generative.* Generative listening and talking can be described as those special moments when you have gained empathetic rapport and everything uttered builds on everyone's thoughts in a spiral of creativity and positive emotion – a place where people's concept of time appears to alter and the normal distance between people disappears. The group operates as one entity and the contributions are so connected that new properties of the conversation emerge, generating new perspectives, and the thinking of the group changes. It is at this moment that limiting beliefs, individual boundaries, and values shift, and a new form of communication happens, where new ideas and new worlds of understanding are created or discovered. Usually, generative discussions are exhilarating and create new understandings and paradigms.

Lesson 10

Mode four leaders engage in pull influence rather than push influencing practices. The difference is that in the latter the intention is to influence for the purpose of getting another to do, or not do, something, change their mind, or force some action on them that is already in the mind of the influencer. In contrast, pull influence is achieved by moving beside a person, understanding their outlook, and then helping them to learn to think in new ways and see new worlds by asking questions and engaging in generative dialogue and listening without an agenda so as to *openly* explore issues and expose assumptions and logical inconsistencies. The important distinction here is that the pull influencer listens and learns with the other people.

Lesson 11

The most important rule that generative leaders follow is that they only use those rules that are useful to the particular situation. They constantly question rules and are particularly good at exposing the assumptions that underpin rules and regulations and feel free to break those that don't add to the situation at hand. These are eternally pragmatic and explorative people who will appraise the expediency of any decree regardless.

This chapter describes some of the creative tools and defines some of the processes that can be employed to explore, reframe, and deal with any ambiguity and provide leaders with an array of options and opportunities in any situation. Based on the creative problem-solving process, this chapter examines the role and skills of divergent and convergent thinking for exploring ambiguous situations and producing opportunities.

As a situation moves along the ambiguity continuum toward total ambiguity and away from certainty, the degrees of freedom that one has in the responses available increase. For example, if you are certain about a situation, have all the data and as a result know what to do next and can accurately predict the result, you have no degree of freedom in your response to the situation. In such a situation, there is only really one rational and logical choice if you want the desired outcome.

If, however, you find yourself in a risk situation, so that there is a risk that the actions you take will not result in the outcome you intend, you now have some degree of freedom to take a different action to reduce the risk. So the higher the level of ambiguity, the greater the degree of freedom that exists to try different responses to the situation. Experimentation in low data situations increases the amount of data available. If you don't know very much about a particular situation, exploration will help to gather data to develop some understanding about the situation. The proposition here therefore is that the more ambiguous the situation, the greater the experimentation and exploration required to understand the situation. The more ambiguous the situation, the greater the need for exploration and therefore there is a corresponding, increasing need for creativity in the situation. The rationale for this is that the closer toward total ambiguity a situation is, the less likely that the rules of the situation are related to previous rules. In order to discover new rules, new paradigms of thinking are required, increasing the need for nonstandard logic, in other words, increasing the need for creativity. New worlds require new thinking, new ways of being creative.

The other aspect of this is that generative leaders, who create complexity and explore the resultant emergent properties, need to be creative and flexible to be able to embrace whatever comes up and not try to control the situation based on some pre-judgment or other.

The tools of creativity are important when dealing with any level of ambiguity, first to help to learn what we can about the situation, for example by reframing the problem definition as described previously, and second, in creating complexity and remaining flexible and being creative enough to know how to gain advantage from the subsequent emergent properties or even just to identify or actually create the emergent properties themselves.

Some tools you might find useful to increase your creativity to enable you to deal with ambiguity follow.

How to find facts

Facts come in many shapes and sizes. Have you ever convinced yourself, for instance, that someone didn't like you? That every scrap of evidence pointed to the same conclusion? You were so convinced that it became a fact that the person didn't like you? Only to find sometime in the future that you had misread the signs and made an awful assumption, that the person does actually like you? The point here is that facts are slippery things.

As discussed in Chapter 3, facts are really just arguments based on evidence and good evidence needs to be both valid and reliable. This means that what we take to be a fact is often only an opinion based on incomplete evidence, usually perceived following the distortions, deletions, and generalizations we make daily without knowing it. The first trick here is to learn to suspend judgment on anything that might be evidence. The number one factor likely to kill creativity before it has even started is to prejudge the evidence and decide what something means without exploring it properly. Sticking to the question, "What else could this mean?" will help to prevent prejudgment. You may think you know what something means or what the problem is, but you could be wrong. The urge to jump to a judgment and find a quick solution is often overwhelming – but don't be fooled by a quick and easy solution that might appear to make the issue disappear. Ask questions to collect facts without prejudging. Remember Lieutenant Colombo in the old TV series. He could ask the dumbest questions with perfect innocence. That's how creative leaders ask questions, often questioning the most obvious concepts and beliefs.

Problem definition

As discussed in Chapter 7, the problem definition is possibly the most important part of the whole process. If you have the wrong problem definition, you can come up with the best solution in the world, but it will be to the wrong problem. To redefine a problem, asking the following questions will help to prevent prejudgment:

■ "What might this problem be a symptom of?"

■ "What are all the other ways I might define this problem?"

■ "Why does this problem exist?"

The idea here is to get as many problem definitions as possible. Include every problem statement you come up with, no matter how daft (a judgment) they might appear. You never know which one might be the real problem – remember the lift story in Chapter 7. Once you discover the problem you think is the base problem, restate the problem into a problem statement like, "In what ways might we ...?" or "How might we ...?" for example. Such a problem definition presupposes many answers, which is what we want. To prejudge the first workable answer or solution now would be a mistake, there might be a better solution just waiting to be discovered.

Idea generating

The next stage after having chosen a problem definition (or more if you are really flexible!) is to generate solution ideas. Again, a generative process helps here, known as "divergent thinking." This means coming up with as divergent and diverse a list of ideas as possible.

The idea of electronically tagging criminals came from a creative problem-solving session in Belgium in the 1980s, involving police officers, criminologists, and a diverse mix of other people. One of the solutions to the question about how to prevent recidivism was to paint all convicted criminals bright green so that they could be spotted in a crowd and kept tabs on. This idea, with many others, was worked on and eventually developed into the concepts and products involved in electronic tagging which keeps track of many convicted criminals.

Never prejudge and dismiss an idea before it has been fully explored, you never know what it could become. The key here is to have fun, play lots, and generate lots of ideas that might solve the problem. The crazier and more humorous the ideas, the better. Such crazy and silly ideas are usually the ones that lead to the more radical new world ideas that move things forward in leaps and bounds.

Suspend the old world rules – maybe they can be changed later. The biggest challenge to creative thinking and the exploration of new worlds comes from the "experts." To be truly creative, these people have to "forget" what they know. All too often, experts cannot creatively solve the problems in their field because the old world rules and knowledge are ingrained. Many breakthroughs have come from novices not experts, for example the Wright brothers were not experts in aviation – they were bicycle mechanics. The thing is that novices often have the advantage over experts in that they don't know "that it can't be done." This is why it is often new businesses that create the disruptive technologies and business models that topple the "big boys."

Solution finding

Once you have your large list of divergently created and explored possible solutions, there then comes a more convergent critical process to explore the ideas' usefulness for the current situation. Start by describing the criteria that the best solution might have. These might include aspects like cost, time, and/or outcome. Then work through all the ideas and rate them using your criteria for best fit. Find three or five of the ideas that best suit the situation; re-examine your assumptions about each idea and then pick the one you decide will provide the biggest advantage. Don't throw the other ideas away; they may be useful as backup ideas in case the first choice doesn't work as needed. Also you now have a pool of possibilities that might just yield additional advantages. Now is the time to use the experts to help to evaluate the solutions, as long as they don't have a vested interest in old world solutions.

Acceptance and action

It's all very well to come up with great new world ideas and solutions, but how do you convince others, particularly mode one and two individuals, that it is the best way forward, as usually such ideas mean change and mode one individuals particularly are largely resistant to change?

This is where the influencing skills of cooperative and generative leaders really come into play. One way such leaders influence others is to involve people in the process of developing the ideas from the beginning – this gives them ownership. If you can't do this, then the solution(s) and their advantages usually need to be demonstrated. Normally, once people have experienced a solution working, they will be convinced.

An example here might serve as an illustration.

After Art Fry[1] invented the Post-it note from the original mistake of the nonsticky glue discovered by Dr. Spence Silver in 1968, he found that he couldn't convince the 3M research or marketing departments to buy into his product idea. So he went away and did some thinking. He realized that he had to demonstrate the need for the product. So he asked himself, "Who will this product help?" After some time, he had his answer – secretaries. To test this theory, he sent free samples of his handmade Post-it notes to secretaries across North America, with the phone number of the head of marketing so that they could call him to order more. It wasn't long before the marketing manager was busy fielding calls for a product that he, with all his marketing expertise, had prejudged to have little commercial potential. The Post-it note has become 3M's most successful and profitable product ever.

In the age of increasing specialization and expertise, it is tempting to believe that knowledge is power. Remember the words of Einstein who said, "Imagination is more important than knowledge."

10 Developing Ambiguity Acuity

Neurosis is the inability to tolerate ambiguity. **Sigmund Freud, Moravian psychiatrist (1856–1939)**

This chapter examines the variety of techniques and attitudes that leaders can personally develop to give them the advantage in all ambiguous situations. These include:

■ Reframing

■ Broadbanding

■ Being inquisitive

■ Developing playfulness

■ Exploring different maps of the world/emotional intelligence

■ Asking questions to blow linguistic/logical ambiguity

■ Levels of abstraction and learning

■ State management

■ Developing a CPS orientation

■ Nonproblem-oriented generative method

Imagine a world where there are levels or systems of thinking, each level having its own values, conditions of existence, and problems that it sees, hears, and perceives. So, one level, for example the dilemma Polaroid faced in the late 1990s, would suggest solutions somewhat like those it tried. Yet at another level, the system of thinking employed by a company would see and value the problem differently or maybe not even see the issue as a problem and would therefore employ different solutions.

Increasing broadbanding, developing a diversity orientation, and decreasing prejudgment

The first set of complementary skills to master in order to develop ambiguity acuity is broadbanding, increasing one's latitude to diversity, and decreasing prejudgment. These three abilities all work together to give generative leaders their openness to perceive new world realities, accept new situations, and explore all new ideas for the opportunities they present with ease.

The ability to suspend judgment until a situation, person, idea, or setting has been fully explored for possibilities is crucial to this endeavor. Often good ideas are hastily criticized and prematurely killed off before they have been fully explored, useful creative people can be unjustly disapproved of and sidelined before their contribution is properly investigated, and emerging properties, from situations submerged under prejudices, egos, power plays or fear, and good possibilities missed. Many people, when they come up against a new scenario or idea, will instantly, and without thinking, form an opinion about it, especially if it is beyond their experience, creates a negative emotion, or hits on an area of prejudice. For example, most people will, if an idea comes from a person they dislike, immediately downgrade the idea or even dismiss it completely because of where it came from. Generative leaders, on the other hand, will give the idea equal weighting and explore it extensively for all the possibilities it presents. The idea gets primacy, not from where it originates. Only when the idea has been properly explored for the potential it holds will the possibilities be evaluated for worth, applicability, and merit.

The keys to suspending judgment are, first, to realize that many new ideas at first appear to be odd or bizarre. The idea that there would ever be any need for more than a few computers in the world was just crazy, or that the newfangled horseless carriages would ever catch on, or why on earth, when you are trying to produce a new super glue, would you ever want to keep an adhesive that simply peels off any surface (Post-it notes)?

The second is to recognize and acknowledge any negative emotions that arise when confronted with any situation. This is usually a sign that you are probably busy filtering, distorting, and deleting data without even knowing it. When you become aware of a negative emotion, this is the signal to listen harder, ask more open questions, and generally explore more. The more uncomfortable you are, the more you need to openly explore the situation. There is a direct correlation between discomfort and the amount and breadth of information you will be accepting at any moment in time. You will find that you are concentrating on those elements that are causing the discomfort and largely ignoring all the other data available. Strangely, the same is true at the other end of the spectrum; the more you think you know what is happening, the more you will be filtering for and no doubt finding the things that back up your view of the world.

The next characteristic on the road to having great ambiguity acuity is being inquisitive. An explorative and questioning mindset places a person into a space of continual interest in almost everything around them. Generative leaders have a broad set of interests and can be fascinated by almost anything. The reason for this appears to be that they have a genuine sense of wonder about how things work, how they relate, and what else they can discover. So, far from finding new situations, ideas, and people a threat, these people constantly seek out the new ideas, gravitate toward new people, and show genuine interest in them, trying to find out what they can about how they view the world and what fresh and different thoughts they have. They will also try new places, taste new foods, or be one of the first to see a new exhibition. They also collect new arguments, reading widely, listening to alternative points of view to discover new thinking and test their own thoughts. Rarely bored, generative leaders will always find something to ponder and play with in any situation.

Playfulness

Another great way to develop a healthy orientation toward ambiguity is to play with ideas and situations. Generative leaders have a great capacity for play. Watch any child play and you will see the inherent genius of creativity and opportunism at work. A table can become a pirate ship, a house, or an operating table for example.

What children are doing when they play is seeking out new meanings for everyday objects and settings. They are total opportunists and can turn almost any situation to their advantage through play. Unfortunately the creativity of play is all too frequently lost as we grow older. Those who retain or rediscover the power of play will uncover a whole new world hidden from those who don't play. Play requires the suspension of disbelief and judgment to work well, the founding attributes of creativity, innovation, and the discovery of new paradigms of thinking.

In the latter part of 2005, I ran a play day for a group of hospitality managers from a hotel chain in the UK. The hotel, like many other similar businesses in the sector, works on small margins and increasingly fluctuating trade. The hotel's senior manager, during my briefing before the play day, stated, "It's a really difficult time. In the past we used to be able to predict when the busier and slower times were going to be. Every hotel in the area had similar business profiles and we could plan events and deals for the slower business months and increase our prices for the busier periods. These would be published well ahead so that when our customers booked, they would either be doing so because of a deal, usually the pensioners, or because it was the holidays, and so on. This year has been very strange. We now get peaks and troughs in a way we can't predict anymore. Take this last summer for example; usually we would all have a good steady trade before business slackens in September after the schools go back, when we would then put on our pensioner specials and try to attract mid-week traveling business customers as well. It's the same for the other hotels as well. This year, we had weeks in the summer with hardly any trade at all and in November a couple of weeks where we were unusually busy. This causes us staffing problems if we can't predict the trade. It's all peaks and troughs now and these are fairly random."

The play day commenced and the managers were given building blocks, craft materials, paints, colored pens, and so on. It took about half a day for them to loosen up and really start to play with the materials. Once they were playing nicely, they were then asked what the purpose of the hotel was. The consensus was that they were there "To provide food, beverages, and accommodation to make as much profit as possible while attracting and keeping custom."

The next step was to find out all the limitations this placed on their thinking about how to make a profit. They listed just over 50 limitations. Next they were asked to imagine that each of the limitations had been wiped away, one by one. As each limitation was removed, the group were asked to construct a new business in any way they felt they wanted to. By the end of the day, this group of managers generated over 700 profitable ways forward by playing and "making real." As this book is being written, the hotel is now engaged in a process of evaluating the ideas through a series of pilots. The first three ideas together produced more income than the last two quarters' revenue combined and they still had a bank of 697 ideas left to play with. The legacy of this play day and some small follow-ups is a constant stream of playful ideas that are providing ever more opportunities for the hotel, the only hotel in the area with such consistent growth. The other hotels watch this one keenly to follow its ideas. No sooner than all the rest move on an idea, this place brings out something new and remains the leader, all through play and broadbanding – anything and everything is considered, played with. A side effect of this has been reduced staff turnover and a happier workforce, which the customers notice and comment on, which in turn is increasing the percentage of repeat business and personal recommendations. Play is creating a business leader.

Exploring different maps of the world

An important method of developing ambiguity acuity is to fully explore how others view the world and get "inside" their ideas.

One leader, Colin, used to seek out people in his organization who appeared to think differently. He often sought out those who appeared to be different, out of place, or just plain odd and tried to understand how they saw things and what ideas they had. For example, one head of department had mentioned to him a worker he was experiencing problems with. This worker, Marie, regularly took shortcuts when applying procedures, rarely stuck to policy guidelines, and broke a number of departmental rules. She was getting a name with her co-workers and due to her abrupt

personal style had become a bit of an outcast. The head of
department had tried to correct the worker, which met with
limited success and usually within a few weeks she had found
another law to flout. Her manager got the impression that she was
lazy and "tried it on" and in desperation mentioned the problems
he was having to the group leader during a regular senior
management meeting. "No one likes her very much, she keeps
breaking policy and taking shortcuts. I think that we need to find a
way to get rid of her."

Intrigued, the leader went onto the shop floor the next day and
asked a couple of the workers to teach him how to do their job.
They all stuck to the laid-down procedures until he got to the
problem worker. The first thing she showed him was how it was
meant to be done. Then she suggested a shortcut. The leader
started to ask genuine questions, like where she was from, what she
had done before, how she liked her job, what she thought of the
current work system and what she would do if she was in charge
(note – no judgment was made or communicated at all, the
questions were asked without a hint of wrongdoing). At first her
answers were abrupt and uninviting. It took some time to build
enough rapport to ask the later questions but as Colin persevered,
Marie softened and appeared to warm to him. She slowly started to
open up. It turned out that Marie had been self-employed, running a
shop for seven years before working for this manufacturer. It also
transpired that she had a good university degree in engineering and
was a member of Mensa. She explained to Colin that the enjoyment
she got from the job she was doing was that she had discovered
ways to work faster but was being held back by the departmental
policies and procedures. Every time she tried something new, her
immediate line manager used the rules to stop what she was doing.
"Without this playing I would get very bored." When Colin
explored further, it was found that a number of her ideas were able
to speed up parts of the process, while others didn't or were
initially unsafe. However, during a series of conversations with
Marie on a number of occasions, she was able to find methods of
making the less safe new practices safe. Marie was quickly
promoted and given the job of improving procedures, policies, and
working practices. She also received some coaching to help her to
build productive relationships with others.

Asking questions to blow near reality constructions

The main problem we all face is that we usually only perceive a skewed version of reality. We live in a world constructed by our beliefs, values, and models of the world. Hidden in our constructed worlds of near reality are a whole series of screens that shield us from the things that are not consistent with our beliefs and values. The result of our near reality constructions of the world is that we are frequently either protected from the ambiguities and opportunities of the real world or we live with false uncertainties and artificial opportunities. A technique used a lot by generative leaders to uncover the assumptions inherent in our arguments, ideas, and situations is to ask particular questions, known as meta or precision model questions, to expose generalizations, deletions, distortions, and other usually hidden suppositions that keep us in our near reality state and prevent us from seeing real ambiguity and hence finding opportunity.[1]

There are three types of activities that help to keep us in a near reality state:

1 *Deletions* – this is where we represent or notice only some of the information available.

2 *Distortions* – here we have chosen, often unconsciously, to alter, misrepresent, or twist information so that it fits with our model of the world.

3 *Generalizations* – when we oversimplify situations or data, stereotype, or make general conclusions without admitting the exceptions to our rules.

Generative leaders are good at recognizing these in themselves and others. They are constantly striving to find reality, to learn and discover. As explored earlier, with generative leaders the learning and discovery is constant. They know that they are only ever seeing near reality and are probably missing opportunities all the time. This keeps them alert to such opportunities that others would normally miss. They are always watching out for their own and others' deletions, distortions, and generalizations that create a surface-level near reality, and they use precision questions to uncover them and get to the deep structure or closer to the reality within which opportunities hide.

There are five types of distortion that generative leaders look for:

1   *Nominalizations.* These are where people see processes as real entities. For example, when someone talks about a relationship as if it is a real object rather than a process of relating. If you view a relationship as an object, a thing in being, it allows you to treat it as different from the people, as if it has a life of its own externally from the individuals. Thus you are likely to hear people talking about a good or a bad relationship. So in business the process of selling becomes sales, or leading becomes leadership, that of deciding becomes a decision. The type of question that exposes a generalization would be "How specifically are you relating/selling/deciding?" Take for example the statement, "There isn't any leadership around here." The idea that leadership is an object rather than a process leads many new leaders to wonder if they have it, instead of wondering what the process might be.

2   *Cause and effect violations.* This is a common form of distortion, where the individual makes assumptions about the cause of something. A common such violation is, "He makes me angry." Another example is, "The market made me poor." The usual way to expose such violations is to ask, "How specifically did the market make you poor?" or "By what mechanism did the entire market cause your poverty?"

3   *Mind reading.* This is where someone professes to know how someone or some organization is thinking about some issue. For example, "I know what they will do, they will move into our market and we will be doomed," or "People like that never buy anything. I'm just wasting my time." Such mind reading often leads to limiting beliefs that become "common knowledge" and can negatively affect performance. Questioning mind reading can be done simply by asking, "How do you know?" The other problem with mind reading is that it assumes that a person, group, or company will do what it has done in the past and does not allow for change. Such activity is likely to lead to a shock, which, dependent on the mode of the leader, could lead to them not seeing the change even when it occurs.

4   *Complex equivalence.* This is where someone relates two unre-
    lated pieces of information usually to support their beliefs. For
    example, "Being late means you are not committed to this," or
    "She hasn't been trained so she won't be able to do it." Here
    someone has connected one fact with another without under-
    standing if they are really connected. If you listen carefully in the
    workplace, you will hear quite a lot of complex equivalence –
    people linking two unconnected states. The way to blow a
    complex equivalence is to ask, "What is it about X that means
    Y?" So using the example above, "What is it about being late that
    means I am not committed?"

5   *Lost performative.* This is when an unsupported statement is made
    to sound like a fact. Some examples are: "It would be wrong to
    close that department," "This would be the most efficient use of
    our time," or "Your ideas are stupid." The point here is that they
    are value judgments that can appear to take on the characteristics
    of a fact. The challenge to a lost performative is simply to say,
    "According to whom?" which exposes the value judgment
    inherent in the construct.

The deletions that generative leaders are excellent at identifying
include:

1   *Simple deletions* are the most common, for example the state-
    ment that "There is a problem," or "We can't do anything."
    Such statements require the naive listener to make a bridging
    inference and assume that they know what the individual is
    talking about. More aware listeners, on the other hand, will not
    assume that they know what the speaker is referring to and will
    ask "What problem?" or "Who has a problem?" or "Who can't
    do anything exactly?"

2   *Comparative deletions* refer to there being a lack of contrast in
    the statement. For example, "Our profit margin is too small," or
    "This is the best strategy." The question is, compared to what?
    So, in the first example, "Our profit margin is too small
    compared to what, when or who else?" The second example
    could similarly be challenged, "This strategy is better than

what?" Unaware individuals don't notice such deletions and accept the statement as the fact it is dressed up as, usually because the deletion fits with their belief system and maintains their near reality intact.

3 A *lack of referential index* is a particular deletion which omits who did or said something. For example, "They say that the market will crash next week," or "People don't like you," or "Everyone knows it's a lost cause." The challenge to a lack of referential index is to ask, "Who precisely?" or "Which people exactly?" or "Everyone?"

4 An *unspecified verb* is also worth considering. This occurs in statements such as "Don't make me angry again" or "You shout all the time." These can be transformed by asking "Make you angry, how?" or "Shout?"

Lastly, generalizations are readily identified by generative leaders. There is a rule they follow here which is "never believe generalizations." The problem with generalizations is that, unchecked, they become rules and limiting beliefs that really do limit actions. So language like, "You can never get promotion here," or "They aren't interested in us," become beliefs and then start to limit how people behave. There are a couple of generalizations that generative leaders challenge intuitively:

1 *Universal quantifiers.* These happen when people generalize from a sample of the population to the whole population, suggesting that there are no exceptions. For example, a statement like, "People never tell the truth," "No one will buy this," or "These cars always break down." The generative leader readily identifies universal quantifiers and will explode such generalizations, usually by attacking the generalization and turning it into a question: "Never?," "No one?" or "Always?"

2 *Modal operator of necessity or possibility.* These occur when an individual uses words like "should," "shouldn't," "must," "must not," "have to," "need to," "it is necessary." For example, "We need to tighten up our regulations" is such a

generalization. The question remains "What would happen if we didn't?" A *modal operator of possibility* on the other hand, is usually indicated by words such as "can," "can't," "will," "won't," "may," "may not," "possible," or "impossible." Modal operators of possibility usually indicate a limiting belief, a state that is the antithesis of generative leadership and as such is particularly noticed and challenged by generative leaders. They look out for phrases such as, "Making that level of market share is impossible," or "We can't do it." Questions such as "What would prevent us from doing this?" are used to explore such generalizations.

Levels of abstraction and logical levels of learning

Generative leaders use levels of abstraction to challenge their own thinking and feeling.[2] Basically, this simple technique allows people to move up levels of reflection and learning. The first element of this is merely to think about a particular issue and then think about what you think and feel of what you were originally thinking about and feeling at the time. You might need to think about this. This is one level of abstraction. It is now possible to continue this process and work out what you think and feel about what you were thinking and feeling about what you were originally thinking and feeling. This is a second level of abstraction. Generative leaders frequently engage in such processes. This enables them to work out their own assumptions and underpinning theories and how solid they appear to be.

Connected to this are Bateson's levels of learning.[3] These tease out the different levels of logic that people can use to learn with:

■ *Learning 0* is where there is no real change or actual learning. While learning at this level appears to be an espoused value, any logic employed at this level only reinforces existing learning and behaviors. Individuals, groups, or organizations using learning 0 to utilize logic that maintains the status quo – they are in reality stuck or trapped in the current system of thinking or paradigm. They keep doing the same things and even when they want change, they will engage in the same practices to try to effect that change. Mode one leaders tend toward learning 0. There are usually no levels of abstraction associated with learning at this level.

■ *Learning I* is associated with learning from feedback. This is where individuals, groups, and organizations using learning I orientations need some form of external stimuli to learn, change or present options. Once such options have been presented, they will then make a choice and change accordingly. Such learning is usually at a basic level of abstraction and direct. X has happened which means that we should do Y. Such learning usually involves making relatively small corrections and adaptations through some form of feedback process. So individuals, groups, and organizations will try one thing and then another, step by step moving toward a solution based on the responses they get in a fairly direct, one-to-one basis. While these modifications or learning may help to extend the capabilities of the individual, group, or organization, they are still within the current logic, thinking, or paradigm. For example, these will typically involve changing existing policies, procedures, or capabilities.

■ *Learning II* or meta-learning is usually associated with a more rapid learning process. It involves the individual, group, or organization in developing learning capability by focusing on how the learning takes place. In short, there is an emphasis on learning to learn and striving to understand the learning process in each context. This means that learning at this level is about developing learning strategies that increase learning. As a result, agents employing learning II can and will create new options, behaviors, and methods if required by the situation in order to adapt to the situation, within the current thinking framework.

■ *Learning III* is a step change in development that little is currently known about. At this level of abstraction, the endeavor tends to be about how to learn about how to learn to learn. As a consequence of this higher level of abstraction, learning, solutions, and understanding are a free-flowing creative enterprise that is not held within a previous knowledge framework or limiting paradigms. The ability to learn and then to know how to develop learning (meta-learning) is enough for most individuals. However, generative leaders can engage in learning III, which gives them the ability to be able to accurately evaluate and know how to use and develop meta-learning. This is a rare skill, especially when this is combined with the ability to do so outside current paradigms. These are the explorers and creators of new worlds, with an exceptional talent to process, assimilate, and, notably, create new information and ways of thinking.

State management

Another attribute that generative leaders have is the ability to manage and control their internal emotional state even in the most extreme circumstances. This entails a high degree of intrapersonal intelligence.[4] Intrapersonal intelligence is one of the components of emotional intelligence, which such leaders also have a high level of. Intrapersonal intelligence is the capacity not only to understand oneself, but also the ability to accurately comprehend one's feelings, motivations, and fears. Also, mode four leaders can, at the very least, control them and in a number of cases can change them to more positive emotions and motivation at will. Careful analysis of this ability shows that this is achieved through the insight that emotions, fears, and subsequent motivations are in reality simply old learnt strategies. Such leaders frequently have the ability to be able to disrupt unhelpful strategies and transform them into positive ones at will, turning driving emotions and fears into positive feelings and thus creating compelling motivations and impetus. This skill is a learnt one. While certain individuals have a predilection toward this ability, others appear to learn it through experience or more formal development, creating an entirely positive working model of themselves.

Developing a creative problem-solving orientation

When solving a number of type II (cooperative) problems, most type III (adaptive) problems and a few type IV (generative) problems, mode four leaders will often use some form of creative problem-solving process. There are a number of creative problem-solving models and the common elements of these appear to be used frequently by generative individuals. While no one model is used exclusively, there are a number of universal elements that appear to be used by such individuals on a regular basis.

Problem definition

The first commonality is that mode four leaders spend considerable effort exploring the definition of the problem and not moving on until they really understand the nature of the issue they are facing. There is an implicit understanding that the presenting symptoms are frequently just that. It often amazes other individuals that the problem they decide to solve does not at first sight appear to have a connection with the original presenting problem. For instance, during the research for this book, I came across a leader who solved a production line safety and process problem in a somewhat creative way by redefining the problem.

The presenting problem was that the factory concerned had a series of hot metal cutting machines which required a reasonably high degree of skill to operate. The process required 17 individual operations by the machinist for every production unit. Due to the complexity and speed of the operation and the design of the machines, it was possible to get out of phase with the sequence of operations.

It was noticed that eventually most operators would start to produce "phase errors." Essentially, this occurred when the operator mixed up two or more sequences of operations. This had two effects, first, there was a possibility of injury if two particular operations were mixed up involving the heated metal strips, and second, it resulted in delay, wastage, and increased costs on quality control to prevent substandard work entering the rest of the process.

The problem as the health and safety officials saw it was that the machinery needed modifying to prevent the dangerous operations occurring. The cost of this was prohibitive. The operators and indeed their supervisors saw it as a fatigue problem, the answer to which was to insist that the operators worked a one hour on and one hour off shift pattern. Again the cost of this was prohibitive and there was an additional problem of training so many skilled operators, which added to the cost. The union saw the problem as the speed of the production line and were actively pushing to slow the whole process down to about half, with a similar scale of reduction in profit. The managers viewed the issue as essentially a problem of a lack of focus on behalf of the operators and were calling for greater supervision and tighter laid-down procedures. The issue had consumed a lot of time and effort to try to resolve.

A new manager had just been promoted into the section and was tasked with resolving the problem which had resisted amicable resolution. Don Gerry was about 27 and was the youngest manager in the company. He had been promoted from the shop floor because he had recognized and averted a production disaster the year before. By disobeying policy, his supervisor, and line manager, he initially was blamed for the event and sacked by the line manager. The head of the production area conducted an investigation, found out what had happened and as a result Don was brought back on promotion and the line manager was dismissed.

Don wrote on flip charts everyone's definition of the problem and asked all the parties their views. With each problem on the wall of the factory opposite the machines in question, he brought in a camp chair and proceeded to sit and watch what was happening. He sat and watched every day for over a week. After three days, his head of section asked him to stop because people were starting to talk, suggesting that the new boy had "lost it." Don continued to sit and watch. He asked questions and really got to know the operators. After the first week, some of them grudgingly admitted that they didn't really mind Don being there and actually they valued being able to talk to him during their breaks and they quite liked this oddball youngster. Despite others' discomfort, Don persisted.

He noticed that the worst operators got out of phase after about an hour on the machine and the best could carry on for the full four-hour stretch without error. It was during one break in the middle of the second week of his observation that he got the realization he had been waiting for. Don was talking to Richard, one of the machine operators, when Richard mentioned, "It's fine until you get out of rhythm."

"That's it," he suddenly realized, "it's about rhythm; the problem is about operator rhythm!"

His next move was even stranger, because the next day he appeared with a man with a long beard and ripped jeans and two camp chairs. By this time, his boss was dismayed with Don's behavior and confronted him on the factory floor in front of everyone. "Who's this Don? You know we don't allow unauthorized people on the floor."

Don replied, "Oh sorry. This is Roger. He's a musician. You are right, I should have introduced you before. Roger has kindly offered to come in to the factory to help us."

The head of section didn't know what to do and retorted, "I think we need to talk, Don. I have given you a lot of slack because of what you did for the company last year and because you are new to management but I'm afraid this is too much. You were given the responsibility of solving the problem of the phase errors. You are making us look silly now."

"I'm sorry you feel that way, but please just give me a little longer. I think I've solved the problem. If I'm right, I can show you tomorrow. If I'm wrong, then someone else needs to tackle this."

Looking directly at the bearded Roger, the head of section said loudly to Don in a strained tone, "I hope that you are right Don, for your sake, I hope that you are right," and walked off.

Together Roger and Don watched, wrote notes and chatted excitedly all morning as the operators worked. At lunch, Don, Roger, and the chairs disappeared and the early afternoon operators noticed Don's absence. Later that day, Don reappeared with Roger, a large set of speakers and a music tape deck. The entire section was watching now as he set out the speakers and asked the operators to wait for each other to start the next operation and asked them to do the operation together as a section. When they were all ready, Roger nodded and Don asked them to start, keep time to the music and work together. Within 10 minutes, they were all working smoothly to the music and for the rest of the afternoon there were no phase errors at all, which was unheard of, and the production rate of the section increased slightly over the following days.

Don had realized what the problem really was. Because of the complexity of the sequence of operations and the simplicity of the actual maneuvers, it was easy for operators' minds to wander and for them to "come back" and forget what they did last, a bit like the experience of driving somewhere and having no recollection of the journey. When they refocused was the moment when things would go wrong. He also realized that the most successful operators got a beat or rhythm going to keep the pattern of operations in sequence. Once he had grasped what the real problem was, it was just a matter of finding something with the right beat to help those with less of a sense of rhythm to keep on track. Roger's expertise with music was the key to working out what tracks to use. They now have a series of tapes with different tracks and increasing tempos that are used for training new operators. The task has now become one of the most popular on the factory floor.

Time

Often generative leaders, while engaging in creative problem solving, particularly between the divergent and convergent phases of the process, will stop and do something else. What tends to happen when space is given between these two phases is that the unconscious mind works on the divergent ideas and adds to them. Many generative leaders have a number of such creative problem-solving processes operating simultaneously, often written up on whiteboards, flipcharts, or in pocket notebooks. Over days or a few weeks, they increase their understanding of the problem and enlarge the number of convergent ideas significantly as their unconscious mind works on the issue in the background. Often the killer ideas are reported to arise at odd times. One such leader sets herself the goal of dreaming the solution so that she will know what to do just after she wakes up. "It works all the time, people think I'm a good logical thinker in the team. I'm not really, but I'm not sure that I'm ready to tell them that actually I'm just a great dreamer!"

Nonproblem-oriented generative method

One method used by generative leaders, especially when faced with a problem, is to ignore the problem, work out what the environmental conditions are at the time and then create a wholly new response that develops a fresh set of opportunities. This is based on the idea that problem solving is energy expended to move a situation back to its original condition and as such, in certain circumstances, can be wasted energy. In these situations, the effort to resolve a problem that is historical in nature is considered to be negative energy. Far better, the rationale goes, to move from the current situation into positive space and seek out the opportunities present in the existing situation and grasp these to move forward into a new situation.

11 | Foreword

Real knowledge is to know the extent of one's ignorance. Confucius, Chinese philosopher (c.551–478 BC)

We have covered many concepts during our journey of exploration of ambiguity and how great leaders take advantage from it. It should be obvious by now that at the moments of the most intense fear, the moments when there appear to be huge threats all around, when ambiguity is at its highest, when we know little and understand less, these are the moments of most potential for moving into a new world and taking the advantage. By their very nature, these are the times when the rules have yet to be written, when there is as yet no operational paradigm and therefore, by definition, these are the very situations that offer the most degrees of freedom to act, they invite explorers and creative thinkers – people not bounded and limited by previous historical modus operandi – to develop their "song's new numbers, and things that we dreamt not before."

Finally, Charles Handy argues that change is discontinuous, in that it no longer happens in a "straight projection of past trends into the future. When change is discontinuous … the success stories of yesterday have little relevance to the problems of tomorrow; they might even be damaging. The world, at every level, has to be reinvented to some extent. Certainty is out, experiment is in" (p. 16).[1] Handy goes on to reason that the future belongs to those who look forward rather than back to history, "who are certain only of uncertainty and who have the ability and confidence to think completely differently."

It is these different thinkers, the generative leaders, who do more than cope with ambiguity. They actively seek out and creatively explore chaos, complexity, and paradox. They are the ones who gain the advantage and move us all into the future – their future. It is these new "music-makers" who are now the "movers and shakers of the world," and who are actively constructing new futures and new worlds right now as you read this – the futures of *their* dreams. The only question that remains is, will these be your dreams or the dreams of different thinker, a thinker who can secure the ambiguity advantage?

A breath of our inspiration,
Is the life of each generation.
A wondrous thing of our dreaming,
Unearthly, impossible seeming –

Ambiguity advantage courses and materials are available from www.centrei.org.

Notes

Chapter 1

1 Arthur William Edgar O'Shaughnessy (1874) "Ode" in *Music and Moonlight: Poems and Songs*. London: Chatto & Windus.

Chapter 2

1 McLaughlin, T. "Polaroid seeks protection from creditors," Reuters Business Report, 12 Oct 2001.

2 http://www.imaging-resource.com/NEWS/995475098.html.

3 Simons, G. (1998) *The Scourging of Iraq: Sanctions Law and Natural Justice* (2nd edn). Basingstoke: Macmillan – now Palgrave Macmillan.

4 This section owes much to the thinking of Kurtz, C.F. and Snowden, D.J. (2003) "The new dynamics of strategy: Sense-making in a complex and complicated world." *IBM Systems Journal,* **42**(3).

5 Schoemaker, Paul J.H. (2002) *Profiting from Uncertainty: Strategies for Succeeding No Matter What the Future Brings*. London: Free Press.

6 Dewey, J. (1933) *The Quest for Certainty.* London: Capricorn Books.

7 Graves, C.W. (1965) *Value Systems and their Relation to Managerial Controls and Organizational Viability*. Presentation to the College of Management Philosophy at the Institute of Management Sciences; Beck, D. and Cowan, C. (1995) *Spiral Dynamics: Mastering Values, Leadership and Change*. Oxford: Blackwell.

Chapter 3

1 Harvey, J.B. (1988) *The Abilene Paradox and Other Meditations on Management.* Lexington, MA: Lexington Books.

2 From Jamieson, K.H. (1997) *Beyond the Double Bind*. Oxford: Oxford University Press.

3 Lucas, C. (1996) http://www.calresco.org/.

4 Page, F.H. Jr. and Wooders, M.H. (2005) *Strategic Basins of Attraction, the Farsighted Core, and Network Formation Games*. Working Papers. 36, Fondazione Eni Enrico Mattei.

5 Castello, J.D. and Rogers, S.O. (eds) (2005) *Life in Ancient Ice*. Princeton: Princeton University Press.

6 Barbasi, A.L. (2003) *Linked: How Everything Is Connected to Everything Else and What It Means for Business, Science, and Everyday Life*. New York: Plume Books.

7 Schwarzbach, M. (1986) *Alfred Wegener: The Father of Continental Drift* (trans. Carla Love). Madison, WI: Science Tech.

8 Waddington, C.H. (1977) *Tools for Thought: How to Understand and Apply the Latest Scientific Techniques of Problem Solving*. New York: Basic Books.

9 Hughes, P. (1994) "The Meteorologist who Started a Revolution," *Weatherwise*, **47**: 29.

10 Miller, R. (1983) *Continents in Collision*. Alexandria, VA: Time-Life Books.

11 Perry, W.G. (1999) *Forms of Ethical and Intellectual Development in the College Years*. San Francisco: Jossey Bass.

12 Festinger, L. with H.W. Riecken and S. Schachter (1956) *When Prophecy Fails: A Social and Psychological Study of a Modern Group that Predicted the Destruction of the World*. Minneapolis: University of Minnesota Press; Festinger, L. (1957) *A Theory of Cognitive Dissonance*. Stanford, CA: Stanford University Press.

13 Simons, D.J. and Chabris, C.F. (1999) "Gorillas in our midst: sustained inattentional blindness for dynamic events," *Perception*, **28**: 1059–74. Available at http://www.wjh.harvard.edu/~cfc/Simons1999.pdf.

Details of the experiments, research papers, articles, and videos of the experiments, including the well-known gorilla experiment, are available on the University of Illinois, Visual Cognition website: http://viscog.beckman.uiuc.edu/djs_lab/.

Part II

1 Alvesson, M. and Sveningsson, S. (2003) "Good visions, bad micro-management and ugly ambiguity: contradictions of (non-)leadership in a knowledge-intensive organization." *Organization Studies* **24**(6): 961–88.

In the interviews, people frequently started accounts of their work and values by making seemingly robust claims, that is, that they worked on strategies, visions, and values, and refrained from focusing on details or directing people. This was seen in positive terms – indicating coherence between values and behavior. However, when asked to specify, managers ended up talking of administrative activities and also referred to the need to be directive, clearly deviating from what is normally understood as visionary and strategy activities. Their talk of "leadership" thus seems to be a misplaced description of what they do. Instead, the managers seemed to be caught in what appears to be almost the opposite, what they themselves refer to as "micromanagement," that is, "bad leadership."

Chapter 4

1   See Heifetz, R.A. (1994) *Leadership Without Easy Answers*. Cambridge, MA: Harvard University Press.

2   See http://onlineethics.org/moral/boisjoly/RB1-3.html for a full discussion of Roger Boisjoly's efforts to have the O-rings reengineered and avert a disaster. The site includes copies of Boisjoly's memos and NASA's responses. While the narrative of the text is necessarily a simplification of the actual events, critical evaluation of the dealings gives an interesting account of mode one leadership attributes in action.

3   Technical leadership correlates closely with the blue vMEME in Graves' spiral dynamics. Beck, D. and Cowan, C. (1995) *Spiral Dynamics: Mastering Values, Leadership and Change*. Oxford: Blackwell.

Chapter 6

1   Ideator: first coined by Gerard Puccio, Buffalo State University, means an innovator who thinks in global and abstract terms. Now part of the FourSight instrument. Puccio, G.J. (1999) "Creative problem solving preferences: their identification and implications." *Creativity and Innovation Management* **8**: (171–8); Puccio, G.J. (2001) *Buffalo Creative Process Inventory: Understanding your Personal Approach to the Creative Process*. Evanston, IL: THinc Communications.

2   Tucker, K.A. and Allman, V. (2004) *Animals, Inc.: A Business Parable*. New York: Warner Books. Based on George Orwell's *Animal Farm*, this humorous and insightful book examines what happens when a leader uses bad management techniques without having the ability to evaluate the technique globally and considering the effect on the system. This ability to be able to make professional judgments differs from mode to mode, each mode incorporating different data as evidence of a good judgment.

Chapter 7

1 By "objective capacity to learn" we mean that the leader concerned will not hold on to knowledge or learning that does not suit the context or situation. This does not mean that they will make the knowledge redundant, but that they are starting to understand that knowledge is not concrete and fixed, rather it is dynamic, contextual, and based on reliability and validity *within* a situation.

2 They will, however, frequently involve themselves in the discussion of the analysis of the mistake and will seek to learn rapidly and creatively solve the issue as part of the team. No blame will ever be apportioned by a modal mode four leader. They will instead engage in systems thinking and try to establish the relationship between the elements of the situation to discover what they can about what is going on.

3 A "polychronic" personality prefers to work with many things happening at one time. They work and think in nonlinear, parallel, and emotionally intelligent ways that let them change their plans at a moment's notice without distress and without worrying about deadlines. It's the opposite of the personality type that human resource experts say works best in organizations, one that's termed "monochronic": time-driven, working in a linear or serial and orderly way, intent on getting one job completed before starting the next.

4 Senge, P. (1993) *The Fifth Discipline: The Art and Practice of the Learning Organization.* London: Century.

5 In *The Fifth Discipline,* Peter Senge recounts the effects of the beer game that has been played at MIT since the late 1950s.

6 The recognition that it is their thinking and resultant actions of trying to control a situation that is actually creating the fluctuations, does not occur to all mode one leaders. Some never get the message and try ever harder to control the situations around them, usually with the effect that there is a high turnover of staff, they are sacked, and/or have a heart attack.

7 Much of these findings correlate closely with the levels of spiral dynamics. Beck, D. and Cowan, C. (1995) *Spiral Dynamics: Mastering Values, Leadership and Change.* Oxford: Blackwell.

Chapter 8

1 Mayer, J.D. and Salovey, P. (1997). "What is emotional intelligence?" In P. Salovey and D.J. Sluyter (eds) *Emotional Development and Emotional Intelligence.* New York: Basic Books. Mayer, J.D. and Salovey, P. (1995) "Emotional intelligence and the construction and regulation of feelings," *Applied and Preventive Psychology,* **4**(197): 2–208.

For more information on the research aspects of emotional intelligence, the Rutgers University website is well worth looking at (the State University of New Jersey). This excellent site includes current research papers, doctoral dissertations, and other articles on emotional intelligence that challenge some of the more prevalent popular perspectives that populate many mainstream magazines and books: http://www.eiconsortium.org/reference.htm.

2   Named after the Mont Fleur conference center, just outside Cape Town in South Africa, where Professor Pieter Le Roux from the University of the Western Cape brought together 23 leaders from the various interested factions before the transition of power from the apartheid regime, in September 1991. The full process is described in Adam Kahane's highly acclaimed book *Solving Tough Problems: An Open Way of Talking, Listening, and Creating New Realities*, published by Berrett-Koehler in 2004.

3   Kahane, A. (2004) *Solving Tough Problems: An Open Way of Talking, Listening, and Creating New Realities*. San Francisco CA: Berrett-Koehler.

Chapter 9

1   See http://www.3m.com/about3m/pioneers/fry.jhtml for the story from the 3M perspective.

Chapter 10

1   Bandler, R. and Grinder, J. (1976) *The Structure of Magic II: A Book About Communication and Change*, Science and Behavior Books, California.

2   Korzybski, A. (1973) *Science and Sanity*. Clinton, MA: Colonial Press; Bateson, G. (1979) *Mind and Nature*. New York: E.P. Dutton. Korzybski first suggested levels of abstraction and Bateson built the logical levels.

3   Bateson, G. (1972) *Steps to an Ecology of Mind*. San Francisco, CA: Chandler; Bateson, G. (1979) *Mind and Nature*, New York: E.P. Dutton.

4   Gardner, H. (1975) *The Shattered Mind*, New York: Knopf; Gardner, H. (1983) *Frames of Mind*. New York: Basic Books. Gardner developed multiple intelligence theory which presents evidence of eight intelligences. This material is well worth examining.

Chapter 11

1   Handy, C. (1995) *Beyond Certainty: the Changing World of Organizations*. London: Hutchinson.

Index

Bold page numbers denote the main pages that cover the topic

CPSIA information can be obtained
at www.ICGtesting.com
Printed in the USA
LVHW081456170121
676726LV00007B/391